NLD From the Inside Out:

Talking to Parents, Teachers, and Teens about Growing Up with Nonverbal Learning Disabilities

Second Edition

Updated, Revised, and Expanded

Michael Brian Murphy

With Gail R. Shapiro

Booklocker.com, Inc.
2010

Dedication

To Dan Turnbull, for being the one neurotypical classmate and friend who actually took the time to understand me.

Table of Contents

Preface to the Second Edition

Dear Reader,

Thank you for purchasing the Second Edition of **NLD FROM THE INSIDE OUT**. When I first undertook the writing of the First Edition, I did so for a few key reasons. First and foremost, I felt as though no one understood me and I needed to tell "the world" (translation: my friends, family, and teachers) my story, just to get it off my chest. But then, the more I learned about my condition, the more I realized that I was not alone. And while on one level, that may have been a relief for me, it also meant that if the "estimated 1% of the population who has NLD" figure is accurate, then more than 3,000,000 people in the United States alone have NLD – whether diagnosed or not.

Those 3,000,000+ people are out there, like me, living in limbo, too "normal" to be "disabled"; too "disabled" to be "normal." And 3,000,000+ people are living their lives with family members, teachers, co-workers, and friends who are flummoxed by what to make of them, by what NLD actually is, and/or who are in denial that having NLD is a legitimate problem. This, then, is the second main reason that I wrote **NLD FROM THE INSIDE OUT**: to tell the world "We're here, we're not going away, and neither is our NLD. Please learn to cope."

This brings me to the third reason for writing this book. Though we (NLDers and our parents) often have read, heard, or been told that all of the symptoms of NLD are permanent, my research has shown that this is not the case. While my book was and still is the first book about NLD to prove this with primary research, I understand that there is much more work to be done, as evidenced by the hundreds of responses I have received, both in the original 2007 survey and from the many emails I have received since then.

I have tried to make this book and the information in it as relevant and up-to-date as possible, using some of the additional information and research skills gained while earning my master's degree in 2009. Though August 2008, when the First Edition was published, might not seem like so long ago, a lot has changed since then that directly affects NLDers. President Bush signed into law a revised version of the Americans with Disabilities Act. President Obama included in the Health Care Reform Bill of 2009 an overhaul of the way student loans are structured, as well as new insurance regulations, both of which affect many of us, and that's just political change. Neuroscience is advancing rapidly, with many exciting new findings in the past two years. New books on learning disabilities are continuing to be published.

And yet, with as much attention as ADD, autism, and Asperger's Syndrome have received, I still have yet to see one novel, movie, episode of *SuperNanny* or "Awareness Day" that mentions NLD outright. But until that day comes, all we can hope for is to be better informed than we were before.

So here are the changes you will find in this Second Edition.

First, many sections have been expanded and re-organized. Each symptom of NLD is now more fully described, based on the latest discoveries in neuroscience. And I have responded to readers' most frequently-asked questions, received since the First Edition was published. In all, I hope you will find this edition of **NLD FROM THE INSIDE OUT** to be even more useful, more inspiring, and more informative than the first.

Introduction

Hello, and welcome to **NLD FROM THE INSIDE OUT**. First I will give you a short introduction to the book, and then we'll just jump right in. Let's get started.

Does this sound like you?

- You began to read on your own at a very early age.

- You astonished your parents and elementary school teachers with your advanced vocabulary.

- You didn't learn to ride a bike until you were eight or nine, and you may have been clumsy in both gross and fine motor skills.

- You've had a parent or teacher refuse to acknowledge that anything is the matter other than your own laziness, lack of trying, ineptitude, or bad attitude.

- You've had a parent or sibling who "babied" you.

- You've had teachers who threw up their hands in frustration, telling your parents, "I just can't get through to him/her."

- You've been labeled as a "discipline problem" in school – maybe not for serious stuff, but for the stuff that gets attention.

- You've had teachers ask, "You are so bright – why aren't you working up to your potential?"

- You have sat and stared at a writing assignment for English class, unable to get past writing the first sentence or two.

- You may have no or only a couple of friends; other kids see you as nerdy or uncool.

- You get along much better with adults than with your peers.

- If you are a young adult, you may be unemployed or under-employed, because you have been unable to find a work environment which matches your skills and strengths.

- You suffer from depression, low self-esteem, or loneliness, but are developing coping skills as you grow up.

Or does the above list sound like your child? If so, maybe:

- You have wondered why he/she is so bright, yet so immature.

- You often worry about your child's safety and well-being, with each age bringing a new set of concerns.

- You have spent hours in teacher conferences, discussing Individual Education Plans (IEPs) and other strategies for classroom success.

- You have (or would like to be able to) quit your job, in order to devote more time to your child, *OR*

- You (or your spouse) are in complete denial about your child's disabilities, and think that he or she should just try harder and "buckle down."

- You have argued with your spouse about the "right" way to discipline this nonconforming child.

- You feel you are neglecting your other children and your spouse, because this child takes so much of your time and energy.

- You live with a constant high level of stress and anxiety, which may translate into physical and/or emotional health issues.

- You often feel like a failure. You wonder what you might have done to cause the disorder, and you lie awake at night, wondering how you can be a better parent.

If you can identify with either of these lists, or if you teach or work with families who can, then **NLD FROM THE INSIDE OUT** is for you.

I wrote this book because, like you or your child or student, I have Nonverbal Learning Disabilities, or NLD. The other people in the book who tell their stories also have NLD. Most of us grew up and went all the way through school not knowing what was "wrong" with us. Some were diagnosed with "non-specified learning disabilities" because that's how we could get into Special Education (SPED) classes. Many did not get a correct diagnosis until our late teens or early 20s. I was 24, almost 25, when I first found out I had NLD, but I had been in SPED since first grade, after my teachers noticed that I was "different."

I was always a curious child. When I was two, I cut open my sister's feather pillow to see how many feathers were in it. I wasn't trying to make trouble; I wanted to make sense of the world. I taught myself to read at age three, and especially liked to read about Curious George™. One day, when no one was paying much attention, I went to the laundry room, and got the big box of soap powder and dumped it in the middle of the living room floor. Then I went outside to get the hose, and turned it on, and was on my way back so I could make lots and lots of bubbles, just like Curious George™. I got caught, and I had to clean up the soap powder. And I was sent to my room.

Being sent to their room rarely, if ever, has the desired effect on NLD kids. For most of us, it's a treat, not a punishment. But back then, we didn't know that I had NLD. Here's what my parents and preschool teachers knew: I was smart and curious, could read and spell, and had an extensive vocabulary. I couldn't ride a tricycle until I was about five. I didn't learn to ride a two-wheeler until I was nine. I was kind of a klutz athletically, and even today, my fine and gross motor skills aren't as good as those of my peers.

Growing up with NLD was a pain most of the time, especially since I didn't even know I had it. I started out doing fine academically, but by the time I got to about the fourth grade, when we started getting papers assigned, I couldn't keep up. I would get an assignment to write an essay, or even a paragraph, and I might get the first few words down, and then I would just stare at the paper. I could not write a paper – until I got to college. Actually, if you want to know the truth, it wasn't until I got to my third college that I really learned how to write a paper. (I attended four different colleges before earning my bachelor's degree.)

It was the same way when I had to clean my room. My mom would come in and tell me, "Michael, you have to clean your room now." And I would say, "OK." But then I would look at the mess and just throw myself down on the bed and cry. All I knew is that the mess was too big, and I could never do it. I would get frustrated and my mom would get angry. I'm not sure if she ever read anything about how to help me, but she finally figured out a system that worked. She made me a chart that said: #1: Make the bed. #2: Put all the toys into the toy box. #3: Put all the dirty clothes into the clothes hamper. #4: Put the clean clothes into the drawers, etc. No one part of this was too hard for me to do, it was just that I could not figure out the steps on my own. We had not yet heard of "Executive Functioning" skills, and I didn't know I was deficient in them.

You'll hear more of my story, and those of others who grew up with NLD, who were 18 to 32 years old when the First Edition was published in 2008, in these pages.

There are other books out there about NLD, some of which are useful. They are written either by doctors or psychologists or parents of kids with NLD. Most of these writers examine NLD through the lens of their own child, their own clients, or their own patients, and think they are doing a thorough job. But they don't get it, at least not completely. You need to live with NLD to *really* get it. *You* know that, and those who contributed their stories to this book want you to know that you are not alone. No matter how tough life may be for you right now, you are not going to feel that way forever. We learned to deal with our NLD, and so will you.

We want your parents and teachers to know that you *are* trying hard, that your problems have a biological basis, and that you have to work *a lot* harder than most people, which is why you might get tired and frustrated often.

So here is what you will find in **NLD FROM THE INSIDE OUT.** In Chapter One, I give an overview of what a Learning Disability is and what NLD is. In addition, I present a short history of NLD, going back to the late 1960s, when it was first named, as well as some theories about why it seems that today more kids than ever before may have NLD. Chapter Two gives a more in-depth definition of NLD. Here you will learn about how to tell the difference between NLD and other learning disabilities, how NLD is diagnosed, and whether the diagnostic tests are really as fair and objective as they are designed to be. Finally, Chapter Two gives a symptom-by-symptom overview of the findings from the surveys and interviews conducted for this book. Chapter Three, "Your NLD Brain" presents an overview of what is actually going on inside your brain. Here I have tried to clarify and explain the neurological basis of many of the most common NLD symptoms. Please understand that because neuroscience is advancing so rapidly, this information may be out-of-date even by the time you read this chapter. Still, I hope to offer you a new understanding of what we can glean about NLD from a scientific perspective.

Chapter Four is called, "It's All in Your Head – Or Is It?" In this chapter, I give several examples of the everyday stress of living with NLD, tell how this stress can lead to learned helplessness, and discuss the fact that you become more resilient as you get older. Chapter Five, specifically for parents and teachers, offers a glimpse into what life is really like for those of us with NLD, plus what we need you to know.

In Chapter Six, dozens of young adults with NLD share some advice about things that were frustrating and puzzling for us. We talk about how we worked out these problems, and/or tell you where we found some answers. In this chapter, I also answer the most commonly-asked questions I received in response to the First Edition of this book. And in Chapter Seven, "It's a Wonderful Life – Even with NLD," you will hear what we consider to be the elements of a good life, plus what we wish we'd known earlier, and what we want you to know now – to give you a head start on making your life better.

How This Book Began

NLD FROM THE INSIDE OUT started out as a 15-page final paper for a psychology class I took in 2004 at Clark University in Worcester, Massachusetts. When I later decided to expand the paper into my senior thesis, I realized that not only did it need a lot more research; it needed some real street cred. So I found and interviewed five students with NLD, aged 17-24. I asked them twelve questions about what it was really like to have NLD, such as: "What has been the most frustrating for you in terms of having NLD?" "When did you first get the impression that you might be different?" and "If you could tell your previous teachers one thing they should know about NLD, what would that be?"

The results were quite amazing: these NLD students, who ordinarily had such a hard time communicating their feelings (a common trait of NLD), who generally felt that no one could understand them, completely opened up to me as we talked, because I was a fellow "NLDer." Through talking with and observing them, I could tell that they really needed to be heard. And finally, someone was listening. They passionately expressed their wish to be acknowledged, to speak their minds about teachers and classes, and about how desperately they wanted their parents to understand them.

When I completed the thesis, and graduated with honors from Clark in May 2006, I realized that this definitely was just the tip of the iceberg in getting the word out about what it was *really* like to live with NLD. I discussed this idea with my mother, Gail Shapiro, who suggested that I expand the thesis into a book. The idea of writing a book was both daunting and exciting. I said I would do it if she would be the editor, because when one has NLD, project organization is a major challenge.

I wanted the book to be for teens with NLD, primarily because I wish I'd had a book like this while I was navigating adolescence (and I know my family and teachers could have used some guidance too). And who better to learn from than those who have made it past the horrors of high school and are now succeeding in college or in the workplace as young adults with NLD?

So I decided to find a way to reach people, both those with and without an official diagnosis of NLD, who were 18 to 30 years old at the time. I created a website, www.nldfromtheinsideout.com, and used SurveyMonkey™,[1] an online survey instrument, to design and post a comprehensive survey with more than 80 questions about what it was like to have NLD.

At the same time, I joined four different online forums about NLD and other learning disabilities (LD). I posted my request for subjects on each of these boards, and the results were astounding. In addition to getting subjects, I got dozens of email messages, most of them from desperate mothers of children with NLD, Asperger's Syndrome or other LDs. Many were confused and upset about their children, and thought I somehow had all the answers to their problems. Some even addressed me as "Professor Murphy," while others begged for referrals to psychologists, therapists, or schools where their children would be accepted and welcomed and would not be treated like freaks. In reading these emails, I felt overwhelmed and sad.

But it also made me realize that the work I was doing was important.

Amazingly, more than 100 people were both concerned and gracious enough to reply to the lengthy survey (if any of you are reading this – thanks again!), and I was able to use all the data from nearly 40% of these replies.

What you will see in **NLD FROM THE INSIDE OUT** is an amalgam of scholarly research and references, my own experiences and opinions, and most importantly, the experiences of many other young adults with NLD, who contributed narratives about their struggles, triumphs, feelings, observations, failures, challenges, and successes. When you see text in *italics*, those are direct quotes from the people I interviewed for this book, or from the people who took the survey. They have generously agreed to share their stories, advice, and wisdom with you, the reader.

I hope that you will read this book and share it with your parents, your teachers, your therapist and doctors, your siblings, aunts, uncles and cousins, your friends and neighbors and religious leaders, and anyone else that you think would benefit from an explanation of NLD. My goal is that every one of these people in your life – including you – might better understand what it is like to have NLD, and will learn how to help you grow to be the best person you can be.

Chapter One:
What Is NLD?

The Meaning of a Learning Disability

One thing I've wondered is: who gets to say what a disability is, anyway, and what is "normal?"

Since the rise of "Politically Correct" speech in the mid-1990s, there has been much controversy over what the "D" in "LD" stands for. Today, many people – professionals and laypeople alike – may refer to "Learning Differences," or "Learning Disorders." At one point I have even heard reference to a "Learning Disease!"

To say that you have a "Learning Disease" is both counterproductive and counterintuitive. To say that there is a disease from which you suffer is to say that you are sick (and possibly that you could get better or somehow could be contagious), which is not helpful at all and entirely misleading. Moreover, the nomenclature of the term "disease" might lead others to assume that you need medication or treatment.

But what is wrong with saying that "LD" stands for "Learning Differences?" That seems harmless enough. Every one of us learns differently from one another, just as each person has his or her own unique personality. Vocational rehabilitation counselor Joyanne Cobb, founder of the Professionals with Disabilities Resource Network, puts it this way: "If we only say that we are people who learn *differently*, then we are also saying that we are not *disabled*. In that case, legislation on accommodations for the disabled no longer apply to us."[2] And growing up with NLD, you need to know your rights – both in school and college, and in the workplace. The Americans with Disabilities Act (ADA) protects people who have a documented disability, but there is no legislation that protects anyone who simply refers to himself or herself as "different."

What of other "D words" that might serve as a substitute for "disability"? I personally feel that the term "learning disability" does not properly reflect the fact that one who has an LD simply learns differently than non-LD students. And while I would not say that the term "disability" implies that someone can't learn – in which case we would use the term "inability" instead – labeling it a "disability" makes it sound as though you once had the ability, but were rendered inoperative. This only begs the question: what put you out of action? Your teachers? Your family? The timing of your weaning or toilet training? Something about your diet or vaccinations? It appears to put the blame on external factors, instead of dealing with the fact that here is a child who has trouble with writing, reading, social skills, etc., and who needs help.

It would be nice if the "D" in "LD" stood not for "Disabilities" or "Differences," but "Difficulties." Yet even then, who's to say that dealing with your Difficulties is any more pressing than dealing with anybody else's difficulties? Perhaps the best term would be "Learning Disorders." That way, all that is implied is that, yes, you have a disorder, so there's something a little disorderly about your patterns of behavior vis-à-vis learning, but there's no real reason to think that you can't learn (either now or ever), nor is there a reason to think that whatever is disorderly cannot be made (more) orderly – something which I attempt to show how to do in the latter chapters of this book.

So why "learning disability" instead of "learning disorder?" Again, it comes back to the legal issue. In neither the ADA nor the Individuals with Disabilities Education Act (IDEA) does the "D" stand for "Disorder."

You may want to learn more about this, or about the Neurodiversity Movement,[3] which advocates for those with NLD and others who are not "neurotypical." For now I use the term "Nonverbal Learning Disabilities" (without hyphenating "Nonverbal," or saying "Disability" in the singular or "Disorder") simply because it is the most widely recognized and accepted nomenclature.

All that being the case, what is NLD?

The NLD "Syndrome"

A classic example of how NLD manifests, familiar to many children, is Amelia Bedelia, a lovable character created in 1963 by the late Peggy Parish. Literal to the point of silliness, Amelia Bedelia, a housekeeper who works for Mr. and Mrs. Rogers, tries to be helpful, as she follows her employers' instructions exactly. For example, when told to "dust the furniture," she sprinkles the furniture with dust. When asked to "draw the drapes," she gets out her pencil and paper and starts sketching. Every little kid with NLD can relate to this, and so can most parents.

But what exactly is NLD?

Nonverbal Learning Disabilities (formerly abbreviated as NVLD) gets its name from the fact that our major language functions, such as reading and verbal output, are not usually affected, in contrast to most other language-based learning disabilities. Those of us with NLD often are characterized as "excellent" in certain academic areas such as spelling and grammar rules, history, geography, physical sciences, some standardized tests, and in most areas that require logic and memorization. However, we may do poorly when it comes to English and social science courses, where written papers are required, as many of us tend to be deficient in Executive Functioning. This means that we may have trouble with prioritization, impulse control, attention, retention, and organization. The lack of ability to plan, to organize work, and to foresee consequences are common symptoms of NLD.

> *I'm not really sure what my problems are, but my bag's so messy, and my handwriting's horrible, and ... they're a little tough to deal with.*
>
> *I'm never exactly sure what to do in a new situation. It seems like everyone else does, but I don't see how they figure it out without asking.*

A very hard question for us to answer is "Why is this particular action the correct thing to do in this situation?" We often have an excellent, extensive vocabulary, and good rote memory skills, pay great attention to detail, and are early readers. However, other language-based tasks often are a challenge. For some with NLD, especially females, math is the biggest challenge.

Simply put, NLD is not like most other learning disabilities, in that, unlike many of the better-publicized learning disabilities such as dyslexia and AD(H)D, there is no identifiable specific problem focus for NLD, such as difficulty with reading or difficulty with distractibility and/or hyperactivity. Instead, the neuropsychological methods of diagnosing NLD employ what amounts to a laundry list of symptoms.

Individuals with NLD are not stubborn, spoiled, lazy slackers – as many of those who interact with us might believe. NLD is caused by deficiencies or damage to the brain.

Are There More People with NLD Today?

Since it was first identified, the incidence of NLD is growing. It is estimated that, although 8% of US schoolchildren are enrolled in SPED classes for a learning disability, only 1% of all children have NLD, equally distributed between males and females.[4] Or to put it another way, NLD, once thought to be rare, now may be found in one of every 100 students in a grade.

So it is increasingly important for more people to understand NLD. As one interviewee explains:

> *Even though 99% of the population does not have NLD, they will at some point meet, befriend, study with, teach, marry, give birth to, advise, work next to, supervise, or otherwise interact with an NLD individual.*

But why does NLD seem to be so much more prevalent today than it was in our parents' or grandparents' generations? Why are there so many new cases of NLD diagnosed each year? There are a lot of different theories and ideas about the causes of NLD, some of which can be attributed to Rondalyn Whitney, founder of The Lighthouse Project.[5]

Whitney posits that there are three main reasons: one of which may be an actual cause, another a cause for an increase in the prevalence of NLD, and the third, a reason why we are noticing more people with NLD than ever before.

The first is genetic. The DNA of an NLD individual contains an accumulation of at least some of the visual/spatial, social relationship, mathematical, and other deficiencies characteristic of each parent; and one partial disability concurrent with another results in a greater chance of NLD in the offspring of two such individuals.

Whitney's second theory is that NLD is the result of environmental toxins, such as overuse of computers, effects of late-life pregnancies, and high-stress lifestyles. But the third – the lack of opportunities to develop motor and social skills as part of everyday play – is the theory to which Whitney gives the most credibility. Writing in 2002, she explains that "30 years ago," most children "ran and rode bikes from morning till sundown. They explored in the woods and climbed trees for hours..." They had many more opportunities to develop their social skills, as well as "visual, proprioceptive, vestibular and tactile experience[s]..."[6]

I would also add that, around 1970, the period to which Whitney refers, there was no system of Special Education (SPED) classes. Those who had NLD symptoms may have struggled, but they were expected to keep up with the class. All students learned handwriting using the Palmer Method, in which cursive writing was taught using rhythmic motions. In English classes, there was no "creative" writing ("creative" meaning "just express your feelings and don't worry about punctuation, spelling, or grammar"). Spelling was taught by rote and students learned to diagram sentences. These highly structured teaching techniques were very, very helpful to students with NLD. And their use may have helped greatly to ameliorate some students' NLD symptoms.

So it seems that the recent increase in NLD diagnoses may be the result of lifestyle changes and teaching techniques that do not give children sufficient opportunity to fully develop fine and gross motor skills or planning skills. Perhaps more importantly, social skills also may not have a chance to develop appropriately.

I always had very few friends. It was very hard for me to make friends with other people. I remember being back in sixth grade. I could literally count my friends on one hand. I had trouble knowing how to interact appropriately with people, which included how to make friends with somebody.

Well, I can say that all the weak areas of NLD have bothered me in some way. But I think the social weaknesses have bothered me the most. I'm not quite sure if that's my weakest area, but I think my social problems have bothered me the most. Although I wanted to form appropriate social relationships, I didn't know how to go about it appropriately, and I got scared of making stupid mistakes.

A Short History of NLD's Short History

You may have a pretty good idea that you have NLD, but how do others know you have it? And, more to the point, how do others know that you don't have a clue what they know and don't know, being as you are you, and not them, you know? This chapter will explain how "Nonverbal Learning Disabilities" became an official diagnosis, and how its relevant terminology developed.

In 1967, Doris Johnson and Helmer Mykelbust coined the term "nonverbal learning disability" to refer to students who did not have a "verbal learning disability," but who were not performing up to par in school, and therefore should be viewed as having a "disorder of social imperception."[7]

Though the concept of a "nonverbal learning disability" was widely rejected by educators and psychologists throughout the 1970s and early- to mid-1980s, some were doing research to find out the root of the impairments to the brain that would comprise this "disorder of social imperception." By comparing the overall combination of these symptoms to those found in other neuropsychological disorders due to brain lesions and trauma, the general consensus by the mid-1980s was that what Johnson and Mykelbust described amounted to a disorder specific to the right hemisphere of the brain.

Byron P. Rourke is considered to be the first psychologist to identify what we know today as NLD. His research and books became the veritable bible of NLD information, and until as recently as a few years ago, many of the books about NLD by both parents and psychologists simply cited his research.

In his 1989 book <u>Nonverbal Learning Disabilities: The Syndrome and the Model</u>,[8] Rourke tells the history of the concept of a learning disability, which he says was first discovered in the 1970s, when he and his colleagues began to notice children who were not as "normal" as others. These children were given the Wechsler Intelligence Scale for Children® (WISC)[9] and divided into subgroups according to the gap between their Verbal IQ and Performance IQ scores (these will be explained later). Those whose Performance score was more than 10 points higher than their Verbal score were labeled "Group RS" to indicate poor performance in Reading and Spelling (as the most prominent discrepancy). Those whose IQ differential was 10 points or less in either direction were labeled "Group RSA," as they were shown to have equal deficits in the areas of Reading, Spelling, and Arithmetic. Those whose Verbal IQ scores were more than 10 points higher than their Performance IQ scores were labeled "Group A," to indicate poor performance in Arithmetic (again, as the most prominent discrepancy, but not the only one).[10]

Later in the same book, Rourke goes on to posit that all those right-hemisphere neurological impairments which contributed to the problems in socio-emotional reasoning in the child with a "disorder of social imperception" were identical to those neurological impairments which contributed to the problems in mathematical reasoning. In other words, according to Rourke, in terms of forming the definition of "nonverbal learning disabilities," difficulties in socio-emotional reasoning and difficulties in mathematical reasoning were inseparable, which was why all the "Group A" children had NLD. In addition, Rourke contributed the ideas that there must be a requirement that the Verbal IQ is at least 10 points higher than the Performance IQ in order for there to be a diagnosis of NLD, and that the brain-based cause of NLD was due to a deficit of white matter (which will be explained in Chapter Three).[11] This was the precedent set back in 1989. More about this will be discussed in the next chapter.

Beginning in the late 1990s, as NLD became more recognizable, many books were written by teachers and parents of children with NLD: that is, NLD as previously defined by Rourke. Pioneers such as Pamela Tanguay,[12] Sue Thompson,[13] Katherine Stewart,[14] and others began to redefine what NLD really was, based on the behavior of their children and students.

In so doing, suddenly the floodgates burst open, introducing parents and lay readers to a whole new set of terms such as "Executive Functioning," "metacognition," "hard/soft signs," and others, as well as many comparisons of NLD to other LDs, such as Asperger's Syndrome, autism, ADD, hyperlexia, dyspraxia, dyssemia, dyscalculia, and dysgraphia.

Parents, teachers, and school administrators began to take NLD seriously, and to create Individual Education Plans (IEPs) for NLD students.

More recently, new information arrived on the scene from clinical social worker Joseph Palombo. His 2006 book, <u>Nonverbal Learning Disabilities: A Clinical Perspective,</u>[15] radically revamped the definition of NLD with his "Theory of NLD Subtypes." According to Palombo, there exists a core of Nonlinguistic Perceptual Deficits – a set of symptoms of NLD common to everyone who has it. This set of deficits, he says, constitute "NLD Subtype I." If, in addition to meeting the criteria for NLD Subtype I, you also have difficulties in attention, impulse control, and Executive Functioning, you fall into the category of "NLD Subtype II."

Or if, in addition to meeting the requirements for NLD Subtype I, you have difficulties in "reciprocal social interactions" (e.g. being argumentative, disrespectful, having few or no close friends and/or being teased and rejected by peers), "social communication difficulties" (e.g. not knowing what and what not to say, and when and when not to say it), and "emotional functioning difficulties" (e.g. poor self-esteem, anxiety, and poor self-regulation); to the exclusion of having problems with attention, impulse control, and Executive Functioning; then you have "NLD Subtype III." If, however, you meet *all* the criteria, then you have "NLD Subtype IV."[16]

Lynda Katz, president of Landmark College in Putney, Vermont, a two-year school for students with LD, and her co-authors write that the definition of NLD usually reflects "the perspective of the professionals involved"[17] – that is, teachers, doctors, school administrators, therapists and others each define NLD through their particular lens. As it stands, there is no general consensus as to one specific, definitive way to identify, diagnose, or treat NLD.

So how do you know whether you have NLD, if you have not yet been tested, or if your test results were inconclusive? Read on.

Chapter Two:
Diagnosing NLD

I just wish that when I had been tested, either in sixth grade or eighth grade, the two times I was tested, that there had been some diagnosis, not just: "this is what needs to happen in your school right now," but also: "this is WHY this needs to happen. This is the diagnosis and this is what's up with your brain." And to have someone [to] have explained it to me then.

NLD in Relation to Other Learning Disabilities

I actually wasn't ever officially diagnosed. I was tested but not diagnosed with anything when I was in middle school. I was tested twice, in fact. But I didn't have a name for what I might have until I got to college.

In order to understand NLD, we first need to look at the definition of a learning disability. A learning disability is a set of symptoms, each of which is based on a neurological impairment – either genetically inherited or trauma-induced – such that the total effect of all of the symptoms negatively affects one's ability to perform at least as well as one's peers in some aspects: academically, socially, and/or physically. In other words, a learning disability may hinder the ability to learn or to perform a skill, in terms of not understanding what the skill is, not understanding how to perform it, not being physically able to perform it, not understanding the logic behind the "rules" of the skill, or perhaps not understanding why it should be taught in the first place. Fully half of the individuals interviewed for this book have had diagnoses of both NLD and something else, and the NLD usually takes a back seat to the other diagnosis. As a result, both of the diagnoses may be misunderstood.

Most of my disabilities were attributed to early emotional trauma. Once I was treated and the symptoms persisted, it was Dyslexia, then ADD. None of these explained the savant-like verbal skills, social isolation, or the crippling sensitivity to touch, among others.

I was very quiet and did not cause problems so I was easy to overlook. I was also very depressed from about 14 on, so some of my NLD symptoms were mistaken for depression.

[What got in the way of a correct diagnosis was] that my EEGs are abnormal. People thought I had epilepsy for years.

With this in mind, I feel it is worthwhile to take a look at some other conditions with which NLD often is confused.

NLD and ADD

I was not diagnosed with NLD, but as having a personality "like ADD."

As I look back over the years I have realized that my ADD tendencies could be traced back to NLD. For instance, I was always disorganized, often forgot homework assignments, had difficulty paying attention, and took a long time learning simple things such as basic math concepts and the difference between left and right. But there were many other symptoms that were too obviously different from ADD that I could not possibly be diagnosed with it; I was lacking in the hyperactivity aspect of ADD, and I always thought things through before I did them, so I have come to a self-diagnosis of NLD.

ADD might be considered the "king of learning disabilities." No other LD is diagnosed as frequently, has had as many "quick-fixes" thought up for it (medication or otherwise), has had as much media hype, or is talked about as colloquially (e.g. "she's totally ADD"). And its very predominance is exactly what provides cause for so much misunderstanding about what NLD is. We all (think we) know what ADD looks like: poor short-term memory, impulse control, organization, and focus; with hyperactivity optional. So, essentially ADD is a matter of poor Executive Functioning skills.

There are probably as many different explanations of what Executive Functioning is as there are experts. However, some of the most frequent Executive Functioning skill deficits thought to be associated with NLD are difficulties with: planning, prioritizing, organizing, sequencing, short-term attention, multi-tasking, retention, goal-setting, problem-solving, and impulse control.

Even this list sounds overwhelming to someone with NLD. To make it easier, I'll suggest that what Executive Functioning really boils down to is the extent to which the brain can figure out:

- What to attend to

- When to attend to it

- How much can be remembered at once

- How long any given piece of information should be retained, and

- How to retain it.

"But, wait!" you might say, "These are Executive Functioning areas that are associated with ADD *and* NLD?!" Yes, that's right – both have the same areas of difficulty. In fact, one interviewee answered the question "What does NLD mean to you?" as follows:

> *Well, usually when I have the different thought processes, it's something that's been going through inside my mind, rather than something I see on the outside, [here he waves his hand, gesturing a dismissal] then, it's difficulty with academics. And possibly with organizational thought. I guess that's something I forgot. Organizational difficulties, yeah, definitely.*

So what exactly is the difference between ADD and NLD? ADD is thought to be characterized "only" by Executive Functioning problems, with none of the other NLD symptoms. So, what happens if, for example, you have both ADD and dysgraphia? Then you just have ADD and sloppy handwriting. But what if, in addition to the ADD and dysgraphia, you also have poor social skills? Where is the line drawn to say that it's no longer ADD, but now NLD? This is exactly why I say that the predominance of ADD diagnoses makes it more difficult to diagnose NLD. What otherwise might be diagnosed outright as NLD, thus providing a broader definition and hence awareness of NLD, or as "NLD minus symptom A, B, or C," often is diagnosed instead as "ADD plus symptom A, B, or C."

NLD and Autism Spectrum Disorders

Often, both we and our parents are asked, "Isn't NLD just a mild form of Asperger's Syndrome (AS)?" The experts don't agree. As of this writing, NLD is categorized as a learning disability, while Asperger's Syndrome is categorized as a mental illness in the Diagnostic and Statistical Manual of Mental Disorders (DSM-IVTR), a handbook published by the American Psychiatric Association, which lists different categories of mental disorders and how to diagnose them.

This means that a large part of the misunderstanding lies in the fact that there are different standards of definition, and hence different methods of diagnosis. Whereas a neuropsychologist might arrive at a diagnosis of NLD by analyzing the results of a diagnostic test such as the Wechsler® (discussed below), he or she could arrive at a diagnosis of AS by determining that the subject displays the symptoms listed in the DSM.

The second point of contention is whether NLD should be considered an Autism Spectrum Disorder. The United States Department of Health and Human Services Centers for Disease Control and Prevention (CDC)[18] does not include Nonverbal Learning Disabilities in its definition of Autism Spectrum Disorders. But some experts say it should be included.

I think it is important to hear directly from those with NLD, because it is my strong feeling that *we* should get to define ourselves. So the survey asked, "Is NLD an Autism Spectrum Disorder?" Like the professionals' answers, the respondents' answers varied greatly. Many respondents said some variation of: *"I am not sure," or "I don't know," or "I don't know what that is," or "I haven't really thought about this."*

The rest had strong opinions on both sides of the issue:

Yes, I see NLD on the mild end of the autistic spectrum. I see NLD as having many similar features to other autistic spectrum disorders, and I have related to individuals I've known with Asperger's Syndrome. I also think NLD would get more publicity and recognition [if it were] on the spectrum.

Yes. I have MUCH more in common with your average autistic person that I do with your average neuro-typical. Also many people with NLD, myself included, have serious sensory issues which are on the spectrum. Calling it an LD makes people think it only exists in school. When I say it is an ASD, people understand more and understand how hard stuff can be for me.

No. I don't. Because if it were only the case that the aspect of social cue misreading was in question, then you could base an entire spectrum of disorders around that, but calling it an ASD is insinuating that to be NLD, you are "somewhat autistic," and that's not only a misnomer, it's grossly misleading.

No. NLD has some similar characteristics but is different.

The ONLY things NLD and autism have in common are the aspects of having poor executive functioning skills, and being "behind the curve" in terms of social skills. But even then, a lot of us with NLD do have friends, and a lot of the time, all "poor social skills" amounts to for NLDers is being an introvert.

I think, if enough NLD symptoms overlap with autism symptoms, the result is Asperger's, which is why Asperger's is so often confused with both. Maybe there should be an Asperger's syndrome spectrum, with NLD at one end and autism at the other. Maybe that might be a little more plausible.

I'm not sure, I'm not a neurologist. If I were to claim that it should be considered part of the autistic spectrum because of afflicted trait x, it's pure opinion. The autistic spectrum should be defined on a purely neurological level.

I used to think that it should and I often fantasized about being able to tell people that I have autism and the instant recognition and resonation that would come along with it. However, I am a part of an online NLD community and I have read some very persuasive arguments as to the negative impact of NLD being grouped along with autism. Overall, I do not have a definitive opinion on the matter because of the overwhelming difficulty of defining the terms "autism" and "non-verbal learning disability."

One answer sums it up really nicely:

No. I think there are major problems with a system that offers services based on people's labels instead of what they actually need.

Gayle Alexander, M.A.Ed., Coordinator of Autism Services for Granby (MA) Public Schools disagrees: "Each year, I grow more baffled by the distinction between NLD and Asperger's. I have not found a definitive answer to this and I have searched for years. For me, the labels are useful in that they give me an idea of what support these individuals may or may not need. Both diagnoses often require very similar interventions and support systems, but it is not until I work with students that I can determine, through trial and error, what is truly helpful."[19]

I thought it would be valuable to get some input on this question from those with Asperger's Syndrome as well. One AS friend I asked said:

The main difference that makes Asperger's count as "sort of autistic" is that in AS there is an element of obsessive-compulsive disorder which you won't find in NLD.

But this didn't exactly explain it either, at least not completely. So I turned to Nick Dubin, Ph.D., one of the foremost experts in Asperger's Syndrome, who both writes and speaks about his own and others' AS. In an interview conducted via email, I asked him four questions. Dr. Dubin's answers are presented here in full.[20]

1. In your opinion, what does "neurotypical" really mean?

Neurotypical is one of those words that tends to mean whatever the beholder wants it to mean. The word itself was originally used to demarcate the line in the sand between those on the autism spectrum and those who are not. However, it is my belief that it is not such a clear boundary. To be honest, I have never met a neurotypical who I got to know for an extended period of time that I didn't think had at least a little bit of autism in them and vice versa. For a great definition of "neurotypical" that shouldn't be taken too seriously, I recommend a visit to this website http://isnt.autistics.org/.

2. How would you complete the sentence: "NLD is like AS, except_____."

According to the neuropsychologist who diagnosed me (Dr. John Milanovich), NLD can be spotted through a triad he calls "Friendships, Math and Motor" meaning that difficulties in interpersonal relationships, mathematics and gross and fine motor result. (http://childmindmatters.com/ProNLDScreener.htm) I would certainly agree that interpersonal relationships are affected in virtually all cases of Asperger's yet I've met some individuals with Asperger's who have very uneven gross and fine motor skills. Some are brilliant artists and musicians and others (like me) can have advanced gross motor skills. Also, many individuals with Asperger's thrive with mathematics.

My understanding between what differentiates NLD from AS is a few things. First, not all individuals with AS have a gigantic gap between their verbal and performance scores on "intelligence" tests, though clearly some do. With someone who has NLD, we are talking about a gap measuring several standard deviations between one's verbal IQ and one's performance IQ. Low performance IQ in NLD contributes to AS like characteristics because problems with visual spatial processing directly effects how one interprets nonverbal cues. Yet those with NLD tend to be (for the most part) auditory learners while with AS, it can vary. You may have a profile similar to Temple Grandin in AS and be almost exclusively a visual learner or you may have a comorbid NLD diagnosis with AS and learn via an auditory modality. Also, I do not think there are quite as many sensory issues with

NLD as there are with AS and the tendency to get involved in various areas of interest and perhaps specialize in those areas seems a bit stronger in AS.

3. What are your thoughts on the concept of an "Autism Spectrum?" What is it a spectrum of?

[This is] almost an impossible question to answer since no one seems to agree on an answer to this question. Some people think the Triad of Impairments is a good way to define the spectrum. But just what is "functional communication," for example? One could argue that individuals with Asperger's have communication skills that some neurotypicals do not, such as unfailing honesty/directness, etc. To me, it seems very relative. The best way I think I could define the spectrum is to say that it is a difference in perception, that individuals on the autism spectrum experience things differently from sensorial, psychological, emotional, and cultural viewpoints.

4. Do you think NLD should be on the Autism Spectrum? Why or why not?

Personally, I believe there are enough similarities between NLD and Asperger's to warrant NLD being on the autism spectrum. At the very least, I think NLD should be a "subtype" of Asperger's. For a long time, I've been advocating that AS should have several subtype classifications because today when I learn someone has Asperger's Syndrome, that diagnosis by itself tells me very little about the person. A person with Asperger's and an NLD subtype would probably act and think very differently than someone with Asperger's who tends to "think in pictures."

So even though the evidence is not conclusive as to whether NLD and AS are the same, whether NLD should be considered an Autism Spectrum Disorder, or whether NLD is a subset of AS or vice versa, but at least you now have far more information from which you can try to draw your own conclusion.

NLD and Williams Syndrome

Another disorder which shares symptoms with NLD is Williams Syndrome. While those with NLD normally have IQs much higher than those with Williams Syndrome, there are striking similarities between the two. Elementary-school-aged NLD children may have difficulty in age-appropriate math skills, and difficulty in tying their shoelaces. The latter can be explained by Sue Thompson's description that motor skills are the main means for comparability. Both NLD and Williams Syndrome are thought to share a common flaw on one gene in chromosome #7.[21] Exactly 25 genes out of 30,000 are missing in Williams, while the ones responsible for the cognitive and social effects number 3 to 6 – the symptoms of which are characterized by "significant gross, fine, and visual-motor problems; [and] dysgraphia."[22]

Moreover, for someone with Williams, as with NLD, there is a definitive tendency not only to miss social cues, but to be overly friendly and trusting, having no qualms about befriending strangers.

Many of these Williams Syndrome symptoms overlap with those which define NLD, and incidentally are the same symptoms which differentiate NLD from Autism Spectrum Disorders. Not being a clinician, I cannot theorize about any causal relationship, but I will suggest that the connection between NLD and Williams needs to be examined.

Why NLD is So Hard to Diagnose

A missed diagnosis is only one reason that NLD can be so difficult to recognize. If your first diagnosis is a correct one, you can avoid years of mislabeling, misinformation, and not getting the right interventions to help you succeed both educationally and socially. The survey asked, "What, if anything, got in the way of your being diagnosed with NLD?" The answers seemed to fall into a few clusters. One was being diagnosed too young:

[I was] tested at age 10, no learning disability indicated. LD was mistaken for lack of effort.

I was diagnosed fairly young at age 12. I first was assessed at about the age of 6 or 7 and was not given a diagnosis of NLD but I'm not sure of the cause of that or the results of that assessment. I am fairly sure that some learning difficulties were determined in that earliest assessment.

Everybody just thought I was weird and a troublemaker/class clown-type. They did not look for a learning disability at all.

Another group said that their early tests showed that "something was wrong," but no one seemed to know what it was:

...until very recently, none of the people who diagnosed me had a name for it.

Nobody – teachers, parents, counselors, and school psychologists – knew about NLD.

[They] put me in classes that I didn't belong in (SPED).
IGNORANCE.

Nobody knew about it at the time. My psychiatrist was more concerned with giving me a lot of medication than with diagnosing me and getting treatment.

The diagnosis may be missed simply because we seem to be doing so well.

I was able to compensate so well as a child and teenager that no one would have guessed if they were speaking to me that I had a disability. I could verbally make sure people knew that I understood the material being presented.

I always got As and Bs throughout school, but when I went away to college, I started failing and couldn't handle being away from home, adjusting to college, meeting people and 12 credits of school work.

Sometimes we – and our diagnosis – may get overlooked because of competing family priorities. That is, our parents also have to deal with our siblings, each other, and other family members. Our parents have their own problems. And they may be in denial that anything is wrong with us, or they may not agree with each other.

Nobody knew how big of a thing the social component was, and parents/testers/teachers did not communicate with each other or do research. The school system should have, under the law, done a LOT more than they did. Also, my parents were busy being divorced and had other kids to worry about. I was quiet, got halfway decent grades, so nobody noticed I didn't make eye contact, y'know?

My parents didn't like me being seen by people they didn't know, didn't really believe in medical professionals. They thought I would grow out of it. By the time I was an adult, I was a functioning illiterate who barely graduated High School. Getting help was near impossible when you don't know what's wrong with you and you can't communicate with new people.

My father just blamed my mother for babying me, like my NLD was all her fault. Until I was 22, he would tell me I had to try to "act normal."

In addition, several of the respondents know or are pretty sure they have NLD, but have yet to receive a correct diagnosis. The survey asked, "If [you have not received a] diagnosis, what makes you think you have NLD?" They said:

A neuropsychologist that I went to for years told me that it was very likely that I had NLD, but that at that time (1997), there was no way of officially diagnosing me in the Netherlands (where I live). Also, if diagnosed, I would be obliged to tell employers. This is why I never asked for an official diagnosis later.

Everyone just thought I was weird, because I can read and write well. No one even looked for a learning disability.

I actually wasn't ever officially diagnosed. I was tested but not diagnosed with anything when I was in middle school. I was tested twice, in fact. But I didn't have a name for what I might have until I got to college.

The survey asked: "How old were you when you FIRST were diagnosed correctly, and who did the diagnosis?" As diagnostics tests have improved and there is more general awareness now about NLD, diagnostic ages increasingly are younger. The respondents said:

> *25, neuropsychologist (male, age 30)*
>
> *I was 21 before they figured it out. I went to a psychologist who missed the diagnosis, then to a neuropsych specialist who got it. (male, age 27)*
>
> *Age 17, neuropsychologist (female, age 22)*
>
> *I was twelve when I was first accurately diagnosed by a private doctor. My parents took me to be tested because I was having trouble with handwriting and because of ongoing bullying issues and social anxiety. (male, age 19)*
>
> *11 years old, school psychologist (male, age 21)*

The Logistics of Diagnosing NLD

The primary reason that NLD has been so hard to diagnose until very recently was due to several flaws and biases in the most common diagnostic tests. How did these flaws and biases develop, and what do they mean for us?

Diagnostic tests have been around for centuries. Howard Gardner[23] describes the unique definitions of intelligence of various ancient cultures, such as the Confucian Chinese and Greeks. According to Gardner, a desire to understand a more common definition of intelligence has evolved over time. Intelligence tests evolved as a well-intentioned attempt to measure a person's intelligence, though because there are so many differences among people, IQ (Intelligence Quotient) tests tend to fail miserably.

Gardner discusses how Francis Galton and his cousin Charles Darwin undertook the first steps to create ways to measure intelligence, how testing was later refined by Alfred Binet, and how later developments such as the SAT or the Wechsler®, described below, became the standard approach to understanding intelligence.

In 1939, psychologist David Wechsler designed a new model for measuring intelligence, separate from the previously-existing Stanford-Binet test, which would

31

include a much wider array of subtests, and thus more accurately determine one's IQ. At the time that he designed it, it was termed the Wechsler-Bellevue Intelligence Scale®. However, by 1955, he had created two other tests designed for children: the Wechsler Pre-school and Primary Scale of Intelligence® (WPPSI), designed for young children aged three to seven, and the Wechsler Intelligence Scale for Children® (WISC), for those seven to sixteen years old. When these tests were created, the need arose to re-name the Wechsler-Bellevue®, and so the main test was labeled the Wechsler Adult Intelligence Scale® (WAIS). In 1981, the WAIS® was revised, and the subsequent version came to be known as the WAIS-R®. And in 1997, another version, the WAIS-III®, came into use.[24] Similarly, the WISC® continued to be updated periodically, and the WISC-III® was published in 1991.

The significance of this test is that most of those interviewed or surveyed for this book were diagnosed using the WISC-III®. (Some who are younger, as well as many of you readers may have been diagnosed using the newest edition of the test, the WISC-IV®, which came out in 2003. This will be discussed later.)

The WISC-III® test includes two sections, Verbal IQ and Performance IQ, and each section contains several subtests. The Verbal IQ subtests include: Information, Digit Span, Vocabulary, Arithmetic, Comprehension, and Similarities. The Performance IQ subtests are: Completion, Picture Arrangement, Block Design, Coding, Symbol Search, and Mazes.[25] In addition, the WISC-III®, like most other Wechsler tests, has four separate indices measuring Verbal Comprehension, Perceptual Organization, Working Memory, and Processing Speed.

The most important thing about the Wechsler tests is the way that they measure IQ. In each test result, there are three IQ scores given: a Verbal IQ (VIQ), a Performance IQ (PIQ), and a full-scale IQ. Each of the three separate IQs was set to record 100 points as the mean IQ, with a standard deviation of 15 points. What this means is that while someone may have had an overall full-scale IQ of 100 points, they may have scored, for example, 110 on the Verbal and 90 on the Performance section. So, while the (mean) full-scale IQ would be 100, the 20-point discrepancy would be significant enough to suggest that the test-taker had a learning disability.

Such discrepancies between VIQ and PIQ indeed have been indicative of learning disabilities. In 1989, Byron Rourke summarized what were then considered to be the objectively observable assets and deficits that constitute NLD, and hypothesized that the Verbal IQ-Performance IQ gap would only increase with age. Additionally, he pointed out brain traumas and factors other than genetics which would account for later-onset NLD, after an individual has lived with a "normal" brain for most of his life. Ever since Rourke designated the "Group A" children as having NLD, it became generally accepted by test administrators that NLD (once it was titled as such) could be defined as the major discrepancy of VIQ being higher than PIQ.[26]

Why might this have been the case? For one thing, one of the most consistent indicators of NLD is that people with NLD have good to extremely good vocabularies. They also, as a rule, have below-average motor skills. However, it is just as important, if not more so, to note which specific weaknesses in the subtests were the basis for the discrepancy. Even though Byron Rourke proposed in 1989 that this point spread would only stay the same or increase over time, more recent research has shown that this may not be the case at all. In fact, they may even converge. In a 1999 article, Pamela Tanguay describes to Byron Rourke the problem she had with understanding her daughter's narrowing gap between her VIQ and PIQ scores:

> Although he personally answered my question, more importantly he clarified the issue from the podium next afternoon at a conference. His answer? The VIQ > PIQ profile, although common, is not always present, since the verbal score may be suppressed by the comprehension and arithmetic subtest scores. EUREKA!!![27]

Indeed, these two subtests, Comprehension and Arithmetic, were very problematic for NLD students, especially the Comprehension. The Comprehension subtest was described as, "16 questions in the form of 'Why do we _____?' or 'What should you do if _____?' to test understanding of common-sense reasoning and social understanding."[28]

In other words, what was being tested was a knowledge of the ability to understand social cues and morals specific to the culture in which the test was being given. More to the point, it tested understanding of social norms relative to the culture of those who designed the test. Because the designers tended to be white, upper-middle class, well-educated males, this might explain why for so long the tests appeared to be biased against women, Blacks, Hispanics, and other minority groups. What, then, is the message one gets from being marked wrong, either because the test-taker didn't understand how to answer the question, or realized that there really could not be any truly "correct" answer?

This problem also was noticeable in the Performance IQ Picture Arrangement subtest. If the test-taker put the four picture tiles in the "wrong" order, yet it seemed logical to him/her, and he/she could explain to the administrator why it was logical to him/her, then would it be fair to say that these subtests were really valid? Or were they ultimately subjective? If these subtests were not valid, what could have been used to distinguish a lack in social understanding?

I know, um...my mom also told me that this one time very early on, either in Kindergarten or 1ˢᵗ grade, that I was taking this test on opposites, and I...was getting it all right, but there was one point when I was tested on the opposite of "thin," and I said "viscous." I mean, granted, that was (sarcastically) "obviously wrong," because, you know, any idiot at that grade level would have said that it was "thick" or "fat." But it just so happened that I happened to be reading, um, this section of a book the night before that was talking about – I mean maybe it was some encyclopedia or something – it was talking about the properties of oil. And it said that, uh, you know, it could range from very thin and watery to very viscous. Yah. (laughs) Well, I'm sorry I happened to be punished for reading something that was not assigned. And that's indicative of low IQ (facetiously).

So, this simply begs the question: Do the VIQ and PIQ really help explain what they are meant to? Why, for example, is Arithmetic included in the Verbal Section? Alan S. Kaufman discusses how there are really seven aspects of intelligence being tested (at least in terms of the WISC-III®): Reasoning (Arithmetic and Object Assembly), Short-Term Memory (Digit Span and Coding), Long-Term Memory (Information and Picture Completion), Social Understanding (Comprehension and Picture Arrangement), Concept

Formation (Vocabulary and Block Design), Verbal Mediation (Similarities and Picture Arrangement), and Speed of Processing (Arithmetic and Symbol Search).[29]

What this means is that weaknesses in the PIQ subtest of Picture Arrangement counted as a double whammy in terms of both Verbal Mediation and Social Understanding, while every PIQ subtest tested for Processing Speed. At the same time, the strengths that could be shown in Verbal Comprehension were not limited to the VIQ subtests. And even though Comprehension is the predominant indicator of NLD, there was only one VIQ subtest that could have put an NLDer in double jeopardy: Arithmetic. So, back to Tanguay's dilemma: although Comprehension and Arithmetic remain problems throughout the NLD student's life, the weaknesses in the PIQ section are more preeminent when he/she is a child. This VIQ > PIQ gap could have closed up somewhat as he/she grows older, and so it was harder to diagnose as such.

Fortunately, the newest versions of the Wechsler test, the WAIS-IV® (published in 2008)[30] and WISC-IV® (published in 2003)[31], address and correct many of the problems of the older versions. So, should you be re-tested using the newer editions, your diagnosis is likely to be more objective than before. Of course, a precursor to any successful diagnosis is the perceived need that one needs to be diagnosed.

And to further complicate matters, as previously mentioned, NLD is not in the current version of the Diagnostic and Statistical Manual of Mental Disorders (DSM-IVTR). Many think that NLD may make it into the next edition (DSM-V), due to be published in May 2012. But until then, NLD is not considered a "real" disorder, and cannot be diagnosed as such, if tests or services are required, because most insurance companies only will pay for services relating to "official" DSM disorders.

Therefore, it recently has become common practice among psychologists who administer the diagnostic tests for NLD to call the results something else: most likely Asperger's Syndrome, or LD-NOS (Learning Disability Not Otherwise Specified), though there may be other names. Because this is the case, it can become extremely confusing to the (otherwise-labeled) NLDer and his/her family, who might not even know if what is presented is the right diagnosis, or if there even is a specific, identifiable problem.

As revelatory as is the answer to Tanguay's dilemma, as helpful as are the new, improved Wechsler tests, and as innovative as is Joseph Palombo's research on subtypes, there still remain some very important unanswered questions. Whatever one might postulate are "core" symptoms, what proof is there that these must be "required," as opposed to saying that NLD is just one big conglomeration of random symptoms? Are any symptoms absolute, regardless of all the changes in life? Do any symptoms change or lessen over time, and if so, how and when? How many and which symptoms must there be, as a minimum, in order to diagnose NLD? Which "symptoms" may be just personality traits?

How Do NLD Symptoms Change Over Time?

With all the hard stuff in my life, in the past, I might have cried from everybody dumping on me all the time, now I have become "mature" enough to be really resilient. And yet… sometimes it just gets so damn frustrating, because no one even gives me credit for THAT!

One of the main things I wanted to find out in the research for this book is whether the actual symptoms of NLD, described in Chapter Three, change over time. What I found is that in most people, some – but not all – of the symptoms can be overcome, compensated for, or reduced over time.

Subjects were asked to rate how well or poorly they did in various areas and skills – **academic**, "**Executive Functioning**," **memory, social,** and **emotional**, such as understanding social cues, and **physical** skills – over time, at ages 6, 10, 14, 18, 22, 26, and 30. The ratings options were "Poor," "Fair," "Good," and "Very Good."

There were some definite limitations to this otherwise ideal cross-sectional, yet longitudinal study. Though more than 100 people responded to the survey, only about 30 completed all of this section. Only these completed surveys were left in the sample for the purpose of calculating the data. So the biggest limitation to this study obviously was the small sample size, which also dwindled with each age interval (there were only three people who were old enough to report on the skills at age 30).

The next limitation of the study was that these replies do not represent all of those with NLD – just those who not only found my website but who were motivated enough to take and complete the survey. Also, there was the issue of subjectivity – not only could anyone enter whatever they wanted, with no way for me to check the validity of their answers, but their ratings of the different skills and abilities were subject to their mood, their degree of fatigue, etc. at the time they took the survey. Adding to the issue of validity was that there was no way to know if the person taking the survey actually had NLD and was in the target age range.

But even with all the ways the validity of my study could be challenged, one can still infer, by reading answers to the open-ended questions, that not only were the NLDers themselves taking the survey, but that they were being perfectly candid and as objective as possible.

In the area of **Academics**, math skills were quite varied, with some reporting always good, some always bad, and some good until they got to Algebra. This finding is in noted contrast to previous literature about NLD, which states unequivocally that poor math skills are a hallmark of those with NLD. (For example, I aced math all the way through Calculus III, so how could I possibly be classified as one of Rourke's "Group A" kids?)

Word skills were reported consistently as "very good," and with one exception, no one reported being "poor" or "fair." This trait seems to be absolute – that is, not changing over time. However, in reading comprehension, the average stays at "good" to age 14, drops, then picks up again at age 26. This may be a reflection either of schools not really preparing us (or our peers) for the typical college workload, or slow development of the orbitofrontal cortex (the part of the brain responsible for focus), or there may be some other explanation.

In terms of **Executive Functioning** skills, for the ability to adapt easily to new situations, the results stay at "poor" to "fair" throughout the age span until age 30, when it increases to "good," and thus it is not absolute. The ability to improvise or ad-lib is absolute, at "fair," while both the ability to prioritize tasks and to multitask improve, with those ages 6-18 reporting "poor," and older respondents "fair."

All of the respondents reported being "poor" at managing time until around age 18, when they reported improving to "fair." Not one subject reported being "very good" at time management. The average ability to manage money was scattered, with the average "fair," but no trend over time.

These data show that not all "Executive Functioning" skills are created equal, nor are they all learned at the same time, save for three: prioritizing, managing time, and multitasking. As will be discussed in Chapter Three, these three tasks are controlled by the same specific part of the brain, the dorsolateral prefrontal cortex. (From recent neurological research, we know that this part of the brain usually does not develop fully until after high school age.)

In the area of **Memory**, short-term attention is "poor" until age 22, then "good" to "very good" through age 26, while long-term attention is "fair" from ages 6-18, then "good" from 22-28 (with one reported "fair" at age 30). Aural rote memory average is consistently "good" throughout the age span, with the majority reporting "very good" balanced by a few "fairs" and "poors," and visual rote memory is consistently "good" throughout. Episodic memory, or remembering what happened in the past (such as where you were when some event happened) averages "good" throughout, with scattered responses, and the majority showing "very good" until age 22. In terms of remembering to do routine things, the results were consistently "fair."

In the area of **Social-Emotional** skills, the ability to deceive or to lie convincingly is "poor" from 6-14, then "fair." This may not sound like a desirable trait to have, unless you really think about what it would mean to always need to tell the truth, and to need to have people tell you the truth. If you haven't considered the implications, maybe you should rent the Jim Carrey movie *"Liar, Liar"* sometime.

The ability to trust others is "good" at age 6, then stays at "fair" until age 30, while the ability to know when to trust others is consistently "fair" to "poor" at all age intervals. These data show that while we actually are able to trust others, we may not want to, because we may believe that others are untrustworthy. The ability to trust oneself is "poor to fair" from age 6-18, "fair" at ages 22-26, and "good" at age 30, again showing improvement over time.

Self-esteem was reported as "fair/good" at age 6, "fair" at age 10, "poor/fair" age 14-22, and "fair" at ages 26-30. These data suggest that self-esteem continues to dip the longer the NLDer stays in school, but that it improves in young adulthood. Holding authority figures in esteem based on their title or rank alone was "fair/good" at ages 6-18, "fair" age ages 22-26, and "fair/good" at age 30.

The ability to listen to others and understand what they are talking about is "fair" at age 6, then "good" right until age 30. The ability to listen to others with an open mind averages "fair" for 6-18, then "good" from 22-30, though responses are scattered at all age intervals. Being able to perceive when others are listening to you is consistently "poor/fair" and is absolute.

The ability to show empathy when appropriate is "good" at age 6, "fair" at 10-18, "good" at 22-26, and "very good" at age 30, suggesting that we do become more empathic and sympathetic with age, while the ability to assess the intensity of others' emotions is consistently "fair" throughout.

Being able to clearly communicate one's feelings is "poor/fair" from ages 6-10, "fair" at ages 14-22," and "good" at ages 26-30, showing steady improvement over time, but the ability to discern the way someone is feeling by the way they are talking (volume, intonation, facial expression, etc.) is consistently "fair" throughout.

In terms of "metacognition" (the ability to infer and understand others' motives), the value was absolute at "fair."

Physical traits vary. The ability to play a musical instrument averages "poor/fair" at ages 6-10, "fair" at ages 14-26, and is "good" at 30, the implication being that those who stick with it can become talented musicians.

The ability to stand or sit still (as opposed to being fidgety) is consistently "fair" throughout the age span. Likewise, the ability to run or walk in a straight line is consistently "poor/fair" throughout, with no improvement over time. Handwriting (speed and legibility) is "poor" at ages 6-10, "poor/fair" at 14-22, improving only to "fair" at ages 26-30. And as for the ability to find one's way around in space, it is "fair" throughout the lifespan, with very scattered results.

What do all these data mean? What can we make of these findings?

The young adults interviewed and surveyed for this book have several traits in common. On average, they have a very good-to-excellent vocabulary, below-average motor skills (both gross and fine), as evidenced by their sloppy handwriting and often, by their being fidgety – constantly moving into different positions or tapping their hands or fingers, or crossing and re-crossing their arms or legs.

These traits were to be expected.

One surprise, contrary to findings in the existing NLD literature, is that only the women – not the entire sample – have poor math skills. High school math seems to be the great leveler, as the rating averages declined over time for both genders, but once respondents get to college, the men in the sample excelled in math, while the women did not improve.

Most had poor spatial skills (though one respondent said that his spatial skills are "excellent"), and in the early grades at least, many did poorly in spite of high effort, which belies their high intelligence, and which may be a contributing factor to the slow but steady decline in self-esteem, which improves only after the high school years are over.

Essentially every trait that has to do with understanding and communicating our *own* emotions and motives improves over time. But when it comes to understanding the emotions and motives of *other people*, those traits remain "fair" across the age span.

As NLD advocate and activist Pamela Tanguay[32] notes, the list of NLD symptoms may be confusing, because not all of us have all the symptoms, and not all have a particular subset of symptoms in the same combination and degree. Additionally, by the time we reach our teens, we are likely to have learned to use other strengths to compensate for some of the disabilities. Is it any wonder that it is so difficult to define and diagnose NLD? To the parents and teachers who deal with NLDers every day, it may seem hopelessly frustrating. If after reading this far and answering the questions in the Introduction, you think you have NLD, you probably do. What does this mean? What is going on inside your brain? We will take a look in the next chapter.

Chapter Three:
Your NLD Brain

It was so important to me to have evidence that I was not "making up" all these difficulties. Learning about the neurological basis of NLD gave me some solid scientific evidence to show my father, who thought that I was just spoiled and was "acting like a fool" to get out of things he thought I should be doing.

Although NLD may seem difficult to comprehend with respect to symptoms and diagnostic criteria, the most straightforward way to understand it logically is neurologically. So in this chapter, which necessarily will be technical and research-based, we are going to look at your brain, at some of the most common symptoms of NLD, and at which parts of the brain might be responsible for causing these symptoms.

As previously mentioned, every Learning Disability is based on some sort of neurological impairment. On the most basic level, NLD is the result of an imperfection of the structure of certain neurons in the brain. Psychologists consider it simply a disorder of cerebral white matter, white matter being "myelinated axons in the central nervous system."[33] But let's first look at what your brain does, what a neuron is, and how this relates to NLD.

Your brain is effectively a three-pound hunk of meat, shaped like a walnut and with the consistency of butter, which acts as a super-computer that controls the rest of your body, first via the spinal column, then via connected nerves.[34] Like many other body organs, the brain is made up of proteins and fat and a few other chemicals (in this case, mostly omega-3 and omega-6 fatty acids, potassium, and sugars), and is part of the central nervous system, and therefore depends on the regulation of blood flow (this explains why holding your breath long enough gets you slightly dizzy – you're cutting off the oxygen to the blood that flows through your brain).

Looking at your brain as "a walnut," each half of the "walnut" is called a hemisphere. The two hemispheres are connected by a strip of membranous tissue called the corpus callosum, which is approximately as thin as the membranous tissue inside your nose that separates one nostril from the other. Through this tissue, each hemisphere can "communicate" with the other. With a few exceptions, the right hemisphere of the brain controls the left side of your body, and the left hemisphere controls the right side.

There is a great deal of plasticity to your brain, meaning that not only does the brain grow as your body grows and changes from birth to the end of puberty, it also grows as a result of learning new things.

The brain has three "layers:" the brain stem, the limbic system, and the neocortex. These also often are called the "reptilian brain," "mammalian brain," and "human brain" respectively, corresponding to the evolutionary divisions of the brain's development. Why?

The brain stem is similar to the entirety of the brain of modern reptiles. Therefore, the "reptilian brain" is about 500,000,000 years old in terms of evolution. It is mainly responsible for regulating blood flow between the circulatory system and the central nervous system, for basic unconscious processes such as heartbeat, blood pressure, breathing, and automatic reflexes. Another main part of the reptilian brain is the cerebellum (Latin for "little brain"), which is responsible for coordination, controlled movement, and procedural memory, or knowing how to do something.

Next is the limbic system – named the "mammalian brain" because it first emerged in mammals – which is the center of emotions, urges, and desires. There are several parts to the limbic system. The thalamus is the "middle man" for emotions, assigning each emotional function to a different part of the limbic system. The hypothalamus is mainly responsible for registering sexual drive, but its malfunction can be the source of many addiction-related problems. The pituitary gland regulates physical growth. The amygdala stores unconscious traumatic memories and instinctually registers fear. The hippocampus is responsible for long-term memory related to finding your way around. The putamen is responsible for procedural memory, such as knowing how to tie shoes, and the caudate nucleus is responsible for many instincts and intuition.[35]

The neocortex has four main sections, called "lobes:" the occipital lobe at the back of your brain, which is mostly responsible for visual information; the temporal lobe, near your ears, which is responsible for auditory information and language; the parietal lobe, at the top of your brain, which is responsible for motor skills and sensory information; and finally the frontal lobe, at the front of your brain, which does the actual "thinking."

Structure of a Neuron, Myelin, and "White Matter"

The brain contains approximately 100 billion neurons, but amazingly enough, these nerve cells comprise only 10% of the total number of cells in the brain. The vast majority of other cells are "glial" cells that hold the neurons together, and vascular cells, which form tissues for blood circulation.

A neuron is a nerve cell that is shaped approximately like an inverted tree. The cell nucleus is located next to the "branches," called "dendrites," which receive electrical impulses from other neurons. These electrical impulses travel through the long, flexible "trunk" called the "axon," and eventually get released through the "roots" to be received by other neurons. In most cases, the axon "trunk" has a "bark" on it called "myelin," but there are certain parts along the axon "trunk" where the myelin "bark" is stripped off, and these exposed parts are called the "nodes of Ranvier."

In general, the nervous system is "fed" by proteins called nerve growth factors, one of which, brain-derived neurotrophic factor (BDNF), is responsible for the production of myelin.[36] The purpose of myelin is to increase the rate of processing information "spiking" along the nodes of Ranvier, and thus to act as a kind of catalyst in propagating action potentials from one end of an axon to another.[37]

The fact that BDNF causes myelin production may seem insignificant at first, but it gets better. A general rule of neuroscience, called "Hebb's Law" – named after Donald O. Hebb, who proposed it in 1949 – is that "neurons that fire together wire together," meaning that when neurons fire at the same time, chemical changes occur in both that link them together more strongly. BDNF makes this happen. Moreover, BDNF regulates the beginning and end points of the critical period – the period, between birth and two years old in neurotypical humans, when one must receive a minimum level of visual input to prevent blindness that was not genetically pre-ordained – and tells the nucleus basalis what to pay attention to during this time.[38]

So what does this have to do with NLD?

Sensory Sensitivity

Some of us lack awareness of the importance of basic life skills, such as how to dress appropriately for school, work, or social events, or of commonly accepted rules of etiquette. We may not even grasp the fundamentals of hygiene, such as knowing enough to shower, wear deodorant, or brush our teeth regularly. If simply not remembering to do these is the case, then this is caused by a lack of "communication" between the putamen and the cerebellum. But much of the time, these instances of "forgetting" to attend to hygiene are actually connected to sensory sensitivity issues:

When I first went away from home (to a summer program), I didn't brush my teeth for the entire summer. I know, I know, now it sounds gross, but at the time, I just could not stand the taste of the tap water in the bathroom. And I didn't know what else to do. Now that I'm older, I would know enough to bring some bottled water into the bathroom with me, but at the time that just would not have occurred to me.

I HATE labels in my shirts! They scratch my skin and feel awful. I would wait until I got to school, then go into the girls' room and turn my shirts inside out. A lot of kids would make fun of me and that was harsh, but it was better than feeling like my skin was being torn to ribbons daily.

This is kind of embarrassing to think back on now, but when I first got my period, I couldn't deal with it. My mother tried to give me all sorts of sanitary napkins, belts, stick-on pads, everything – but everything felt terribly itchy to me and it chafed. All I wanted to do was to sit at home in the bathtub for the whole four days every month.

So this only begs the question: from where do these sensory sensitivity issues come? According to neuroplasticity expert Michael Merzenich, in researching the root causes of autism, it has to do with frontloading of BDNF. According to Merzenich, those with autism are born with a genetic tendency to be much more sensitive to BDNF in the critical period, the first two years of life, than are their neurotypical peers. If, in those first two years, the autistic child's brain is overexcited, then there is a massive, premature release of BDNF, causing the neurons to grow myelin much faster than usual, neural connections to be made indiscriminately, and the critical period to be shut down early. If the overexcitement is auditory, the child will develop a hypersensitivity to certain sounds; if the overexcitement is visual, the child will develop a hypersensitivity to certain lights; if the overexcitement is tactile, the child will develop a hypersensitivity to certain textures. But the fact that neurons are so interconnected means that whenever they are overstimulated, it is as though their whole brain is being overstimulated all at once.[39]

According to Merzenich, the real reason autism (and I would say all Autism Spectrum Disorders) is so much more prevalent now than it used to be – once increased diagnosis is factored in – is that "infants are reared in continuously more noisy environments. There is always a din [...] every time you have a pulse, you are excited [sic] everything in the auditory cortex – every neuron."[40] Effectively, Merzenich is arguing that, as technology advances, and we are raised around more white noise (multiple sound frequencies at once, often rapidly pulsing, that are very stimulating), and more strobe lights (multiple light frequencies at once, often rapidly pulsing, that are very stimulating), the more cases of the critical period shutting down early because this bombardment of input is too much too soon, leading to more diagnoses of developmental disabilities later on. That is probably the best argument for the rise of autism I have ever heard. But lest you think I am only talking about autism, recall Rondalyn Whitney's three-fold explanation for the rise of NLD mentioned in Chapter One: genetics, environmental toxins, and shifts in behavioral patterns and expectations. Viewed through the lens of Merzenich's theory, Whitney has won the trifecta in explaining NLD among developmental disabilities on the basis of sensory sensitivity alone.

Left Versus Right

Clearly, the level and timing of the first increase in myelin is a definitive factor of NLD. But what of a decrease? Many experts, starting with Byron Rourke[41] think that demyelination (reduction of myelin) exacerbates the syndromes of NLD when it occurs in the right hemisphere of the brain more than in the left hemisphere. As stated previously, the two hemispheres are connected by the corpus callosum, through which each hemisphere can "communicate" with the other.

When talking about NLD, psychologists mainly dwell on the problem of the right hemisphere (occasionally in lieu of other possibilities), because it is generally accepted psychological theory that the left hemisphere focuses on the "details," such as math and word skills, deductive and inductive logic, spoken language, scientific skills, and others; while the right hemisphere focuses on the "big picture:" insight, art appreciation, music appreciation, 3-D forms, creativity, and imagination, among others. The natural inclination is for psychologists to lateralize symptoms – that is, to say it must be due to a deficiency in one hemisphere or the other. For many NLD symptoms, this actually is not wrong.

Lost in Space

For example, a lesion on the right side of the brain in the region of the parietal lobe closest to the occipital lobe, which pertains both to being able to see two things at the same time and to spatial awareness (for example, the ability to mentally rotate objects in space) will cause someone to be unable to find their way around in space. This inferior spatial orientation is a problem very common among NLDers and usually at least one of their parents as well.

While playing Little League baseball in the fifth grade, I hit a single. When I was about halfway to first base, I saw the second baseman pick up the ball. I thought there was no chance I could make it to first base, so I just ran off the field. My teammates were mad, and told me I could've easily made it. To me the distance looked enormous, even insurmountable.

Moreover, if the right side of the hippocampus, responsible for "big picture" memory, also is damaged, the problem perhaps may extend to getting lost in the most familiar settings.[42] And this would account for the phenomenon of not being able to figure out how to drive from your house to the nearest highway, even though all the streets and landmarks in between are perfectly familiar.

At this point in my life, the most frustrating thing is my spatial/directional difficulties, because I want very much to adapt and drive well to any location I want, but the fact is that with a new place it takes me maybe a couple of practice tries – or more.

It would not be surprising to find an elementary school child with NLD literally emulating Hansel and Gretel by placing physical markers along the path to help find the way back to school from recess. Of course, this is contingent on the notion that he or she would think to do such a thing in the first place.

Once, during kindergarten recess, I followed a butterfly into the woods, because I wanted to see where he lived. I didn't hear the bell, or the teacher calling me back. No one could find me, and all the teachers and staff, even the principal, had to go out looking for me. After that, the school didn't know what to do with me, so for first grade, they put me into SPED.

NLD in 3-D?

But there is more to the brain than just the left hemisphere versus the right. Even Rourke had to admit this. He postulates that white matter is not just one big homogeneous glob of myelin; instead there are three types of neurons that, when myelinated, comprise white matter. The first set is Association (Back □ Front) Fibers, which interconnect different lobes within the same hemisphere, and on which the left hemisphere is more "dependent." The next set are Projection (Down □ Up) Fibers, which act as the basic input-output system between the cerebral hemispheres and the diencephalons, the front part of the limbic system. Commissural (Right □ Left) Fibers go through the corpus callosum, on which the right hemisphere is more "dependent," and therefore if damaged, would be the prime cause of NLD. [43]

Still, this misses the point. NLD is not limited in scope simply to a matter of being a "right hemisphere disorder." When I first proposed the topic of NLD as my senior thesis to Dr. David Stevens, my advisor at Clark University, he asked me, "How can it possibly be that NLD is just a right hemisphere disorder? It sounds like all there is to it is just a bunch of holes punched out of the right hemisphere of the brain, and all of a sudden, ta-da! You have NLD! That just doesn't make sense."[44] I had to admit, he was right. So I threw out the "conventional wisdom" and started again by approaching NLD on a symptom-by-symptom basis. Here's what I found out.

Talking Too Much

Insofar as the "details" vs. "big picture" approach applies to the language organization area of the prefrontal cortex, it may help answer one of the most common questions of frustrated parents and teachers: Why don't teens and young adults with NLD *ever* stop arguing? Why do we keep on talking, to the point where the listener sometimes just wants to scream, "I get it. *I get it already!*"

Here's why: if the area of the brain containing the language cortex – located in the left hemisphere, in the frontal and temporal lobes – is working normally, and so are all other brain areas, then one could construct a clear, concise, argument. But what exactly prevents someone from doing that – from making his/her point? There are two possible reasons.

One, he/she could know that there is a point that he/she is trying to make, but simply can't get the right words out – which actually would indicate that something was wrong with the details-oriented left hemisphere, while the "big picture"-oriented right hemisphere understands the gist of what he/she is trying to say. Specifically, the problem would be converting the sequencing of individual letters, phonemes, and words that make up a thought into the sequence of lip movements that would represent the thought when spoken. This is indicative of a faulty left pre-motor cortex. Moreover, if, instead of trying to convert the thought to a spoken statement, the NLDer were to try to convert it to a written one, then this left pre-motor cortex problem would manifest as dysgraphia.[45]

The other possibility is that he/she is early in the logical sequence of steps that entails making an argument for his/her (end) point, but the audience already has deduced or inferred what point he/she is trying to make, and the person with NLD, deficient in reading social cues, either hasn't noticed this, or cannot understand how the person to whom he/she is talking has figured out what point is being made if he/she hasn't finished making it yet, and thus he/she goes right on talking, until he/she is sure that he/she understands how to arrive at his/her conclusion, regardless of whether or not his/her audience is actually still bothering to listen. (See what I mean?) In this case, the part of the brain responsible for this critically-important aspect of NLD is the prefrontal cortex.

Executive Functioning: Lack of Planning Skills

One section of the prefrontal cortex, the dorsolateral prefrontal cortex, is often dubbed "the central executive," hence the term "Executive Functioning" to describe its role in planning and prioritizing and sequencing thought and actions. Many people with NLD have difficulty with tasks that require planning, though they are quite capable of doing all the tasks in a plan once it is made.

The purpose of this brain function is to oversee how memory is operating. "Things are held 'in mind' here, and manipulated to form plans and concepts. This area also seems to choose to do one thing over another."[46] In other words, to prioritize.

These tasks are notoriously difficult for those with NLD. The process of setting up and actually conducting the initial interviews for this book illustrates the challenges in planning skills experienced by most of us with NLD. Listen to what happened:

When I arrived at 12:58 pm at the college library, I went straight to stack three, where she [the subject] told me she would meet me at 1:00 pm. I waited until 1:12, and she still wasn't there. Then I went back into the main area of the library, asked a girl sitting on a couch, if she had seen who I was looking for, and she replied, "Oh, that's me!" So we had to start at 1:15. This is so typical of two NLD individuals that we both laughed.

[We] met on the main floor of the library. I waited for him for about 20 minutes before he actually showed up. Since I wasn't sure he would remember the appointment, I had emailed him the day before. When I did not get an answer by about an hour before the interview, I called his dorm room and apparently woke him up. I apologized, and he complained, "Why did you have to wake me up now? It's not for an hour, is it?" But then, when he finally showed up, he grudgingly acknowledged that without my phone call, he would have slept right through the appointment. He was still wearing his pajamas, but with a trench coat over them. On his feet, he wore flip-flops. In February. When it was snowing outside. His hair was completely disheveled, and he apparently had chosen not to shave for about two weeks. Despite his fatigue, he was pleasant and funny and the interview proceeded smoothly, once we found a place to do it.

[For the third one] we had to look all over the library for a quiet space. I first asked the guy at the Circulation desk if we could have the conference room I had used for the interview last week. He said no, so we looked all over the 4th floor for a place that was at least semi-private. Not only did it take us about 20 minutes to find a good place, but we both were getting incredibly lost. We finally started at about 11:45, for the interview that had been scheduled for 11:00. Again, I had to laugh at the predictably unpredictable scenario of two people with NLD trying to do an interview.

It is therefore reasonable to assume that the "central executive" section of the brain, responsible for deciding what to remember, is a likely candidate for being damaged in NLD. Yet once the brain has locked in on what it wants to remember, if NLDers lack the ability to "coordinate incoming information with information already in the system,"[47] is it really any surprise, then, that we are so resistant to virtually any change?

OK, I admit it. Looking back, it even seems kind of silly now. But when my parents took out the 80s-style track lighting in the living room to replace it with recessed lighting, I actually lay down on the floor and cried. I mean, the lights have been that way my whole life. I don't like things to change.

When my family travels on vacation, I have a hard time adjusting to sleeping in a hotel. Don't get me wrong – I really like going on vacation, but the bed is different, the smells and sounds are different, the food is different and that always takes some getting used to. After the first few days, it's not so bad. But I am always very happy to come home again.

It is incredibly difficult for me if they change the bell schedule in school for any reason – like an assembly or a teachers' meeting or something. I know where I am supposed to be at any given time on a particular day, but if they switch the schedule from an "A" day to a "B" day, I get very, very anxious.

Speaking, Listening, Arguing

Speculation though this might be, I would posit that perhaps the reason why many people with NLD have some difficulty speaking extemporaneously is that there might be damage to a connection between the dorsolateral prefrontal cortex, where concepts are formed, and the left pre-motor cortex, which, as previously mentioned, converts the sequence of letters in thought format to spoken word format or written word format.

Without this particular aspect of Executive Functioning, one would lack the internal knowledge to know when, exactly, one's point has been made sufficiently, whereas in the process of making the argument itself, one's thinking will be more "strictly logical" (being actually literal).

In terms of listening to another person, if our language cortex is working overtime, we will not know when to stop talking. We also will be more likely to nit-pick the argument of the person with whom we are conversing because, while we *think* we know what we want to say, we haven't yet gotten our thoughts completely organized. When we listen to someone else, they may be creating a logical, linear argument, proceeding from Point A to Point Z, for example. But if their Point B does not make sense immediately, we may tune out everything else they say and just stick to arguing that one point. We do this even if, in the process of our attempt to refute that point, we don't yet know exactly what we need to say or are going to say. But we have a need to just keep talking until our argument makes sense to us, which can be really annoying to the other person. Absent Executive Functioning skills, we will sequence our argument aloud until we feel we've made our point sufficiently.

And once the other person grasps that we are not paying attention to anything after their Point B, and they then try to explain that if we would just shut up and listen, we will get it, we get even more frustrated and angry, even as we wish they would shut up and listen to us. So what started as a conversation and turned into a debate now becomes a fight. (You parents reading this know exactly what I mean!)

These are all-too-common symptoms of NLD. And the same deficit in the left side of the prefrontal cortex, just at the back edge of the orbitofrontal cortex, causes a reduced ability to infer meaning from what we read or hear.

Reading comprehension tests were the worst. I just can't grasp the main points in any story, but can repeat the details back to you verbatim.

Poor Impulse Control and Emotional Immaturity

Another common symptom of those with NLD is poor impulse control.

Talk about lack of impulse control! I was making a total jackass out of myself in high school... trying to show off to impress a certain girl. Instead, I earned the most suspensions in the history of the school.

In addition to being partly responsible for reading comprehension (which requires the language and vision areas to be competent), the orbitofrontal cortex also is in charge of the ability to put aside short-term pleasures for long-term gains (a.k.a. higher-order planning), a feeling that "something is wrong here," and the ability to understand what actions are inappropriate.[48] A damaged orbitofrontal cortex is responsible for a lack of or reduced impulse control.

It is the combined development of these two parts of the frontal lobe – the orbitofrontal cortex and the dorsolateral prefrontal cortex – that is responsible for the degree to which someone is "mature," as defined by the degree to which they can manifest the same mastery over Executive Functioning skills as their neurotypical peers. This may explain why we NLDers tend to be noticeably immature with respect to chronological age.

Many experts in the field think that the emotional age of those with NLD is about 75% of our chronological age, and my research bears this out. Thus, a 16-year-old would act more like she is 12, and a 20-year-old would have the emotional capabilities of a typical 15-year-old. This is true until the mid- to late 20s, when we start to catch up.

While this may not seem like much of a problem in elementary school (an 8-year-old acting like a 6-year-old is not that unusual, and is hard to peg anyway), this age-based discrepancy manifests itself in extremely significant ways. An 18-year-old NLDer who has not yet shown any major teenage rebellion is actually normal. Parents should not think themselves lucky to have "breezed right through" the famous adolescent rebellion, because an 18-year-old with NLD still has the emotional age of about 13½. So the true "rebellious adolescent" will manifest only when he/she is of college age. Be prepared.

> *My parents had such a hard time with my older siblings during their adolescence, that when I hit 20 and hadn't given them any cause to worry, they thought we all had just sailed right through. Were they surprised to find out that I was just getting started with my so-called teenage rebellion! Looking back, I know I gave them a few rough years there. But everyone goes through the normal stages of development. NLD kids just go through them later.*

Following the same trajectory, we are likely to reach the emotional age of a neurotypical 18-year-old when we are about 24. So this might be the first time we are ready to live away from home in a minimally-supervised situation, such as a dorm, with true independent living not until the late 20s or so. This is difficult to hear, both for us and for our parents. And to make it even worse, the world isn't really set up for a 24-year-old to live in a college freshman dorm.

Reflections on Social Cues: Mirror Neurons

Do you have trouble understanding what people actually mean when they are talking to you? Or worse, when they say one thing and seem to mean another – for example, when they are being sarcastic or speaking metaphorically? Do you miss nuances in conversation? If so, you are not alone. Another common symptom of NLD is a lack of understanding social cues – what people mean when they don't say what they mean – or when they use body language or facial expressions to show how they feel. Not only are these nonverbal communications difficult or impossible for us to interpret, often we also do not know how to respond. An example from one of the first interviews for this book illustrates this point:

> *[We met] in a small coffee shop/bookstore ... we sat down in two big leather chairs in the lounge, and began. I started out the interview with the question, "How are you doing?" and he asked, "What do you mean, 'how am I doing?'" I then stopped the tape recorder, and rewound it. He then started to question me on why I was asking, and what this interview was all about [even though I had previously explained it to him on the phone]. I proceeded to tell him that this was a senior thesis I was doing for my Psychology major, and that I had NLD, and that a big part of my study was collecting other first-hand accounts. Only then did he say that he understood, and I said, "OK, when I ask you, 'How are you doing' this time, I mean it as an icebreaker." He then said, "OK." I turned on the tape recorder to record over the "false start" and we began again.*

The lack of ability to pick up on social cues is a hallmark of NLD. One explanation might be found in a relatively recent trend in neuroscientific research: the study of mirror neurons, first discovered in 1995 by Iaccomo Rizzolati and Vittorio Gallasse, researchers at the University of Parma, who worked with macaque monkeys. While measuring neural activities of these monkeys who were eating, the researchers discovered that the areas of the monkeys' brains that were active when they reached for a peanut also were active in the monkeys' brains when the monkeys watched the human researchers reach for a peanut. It appeared that the monkeys' brains didn't register the difference between when they themselves reached for the peanut and when they saw someone else do it!

How does this story relate to NLD?

Suppose that this (at least partial) inability to tell the difference between your own actions and someone else's actions could apply to humans. What might this mean? Rizzolati and Gallasse's work generated much interest among other neurologists. In 2005, Marco Iacoboni and his team of fellow researchers at UCLA published a study that said that the neurons in the human anterior cingulate, which fire when one experiences pain (such as when one is being poked with a needle) also fire when someone *else* is in pain.[49]

Dozens of subsequent studies prove that for neurotypical humans, information is received in certain parts of the brain when they observe someone else do something which mirrors the information they themselves would get from doing the same thing. (Visual information is received in the occipital lobe, auditory in the temporal lobe, motor and sensory in the parietal lobe.) And when this information is sent to the limbic system, they connect the actions with the usual associated emotions.

As an automatic reflex, they laugh when others laugh, cry when others cry, etc. And when all of this emotional information gets sent to the orbitofrontal cortex, neurotypical people sort it all out, understand what the feelings mean, and why others are feeling the way they are. So they are, in essence, first being empathic, and then, perhaps, even understanding of others' motives. Ah, but this applies only to the neurotypical human...

NLDers can laugh when others laugh, and wince when they see someone get slammed, just like everyone else, but it is the ability (or lack thereof) to understand emotions – not only our own but others' – that's the problem. And it's not just a symptom of

NLD, it also tends to be true of those disorders in the "Autism Spectrum": autism, High Functioning Autism, PDD, and Asperger's Syndrome. This lack occurring in these disorders is caused primarily by a deficit of neural communication in the mirror neuron system, specifically in the connection between the right orbitofrontal cortex and the amygdala.[50] This lack causes both a reduced capacity for empathy and dyssemia (difficulty understanding and using nonverbal "signs," such as reading facial expressions and interpreting tone of voice).[51]

Additionally, the right orbitofrontal cortex's two next-door neighbors, the anterior cingulate cortex and the rostral cingulated zone, have a lot to do with the true nature of social skills, according to new research by neurologist Louann Brizendine, M.D.[52] Brizendine describes the anterior cingulate cortex as "the worry-wart, fear-of-punishment area, and center of sexual performance anxiety. It's smaller in men than in women. It weighs options, detects conflicts, motivates decisions. Testosterone decreases worries about punishment. The ACC is also the area for self-consciousness."[53] It would therefore seem that if this area is not working well in those with NLD, it might help to account for our being over-trusting and for our naïveté.

Yet even more important is the rostral cingulate zone, which Brizendine describes as "the brain's barometer for registering social approval or disapproval. This 'I am accepted or not' area keeps humans from making the most fundamental social mistake: being too different from others. The RCZ is the brain center for processing social errors..."[54] Needless to say, if the "brain center for processing social errors" isn't working well, this can lead to some serious faux pas.

> *Well, I used to complain about things that, at inopportune times, like at a birthday party once, the cake was an ice cream cake, and I started complaining about that, and my mom had to say to me, "Quiet down, it's a* birthday *party." Well, you know, I'm more conscious of that now.*

Other Symptoms

Up to this point, we have discussed many of the characteristic traits of NLD, including visuo-spatial problems, sensory sensitivity, forgetting to do routine things while needing a routine, missing social cues, hygiene issues, dysgraphia, panic, and social acceptance, plus multiple aspects of "Executive Functioning:" impulse control, thinking through how to say something before you say it, scheduling, and "higher-order planning."

This may seem like a comprehensive list, but as the survey showed, there are many other common symptoms of NLD such as: poor gross motor skills, manifesting as both clumsiness and as an inability to sit without fidgeting; lack of eye contact; the fact that we seem to be great at vocabulary and may teach ourselves to read at an early age; and, especially in females, a tendency to decline in math skills over time.

Here's what we know for certain. First, there is a lot more to NLD than a "right hemisphere disorder," because not only does this nomenclature not take into account "Executive Functioning skills," the roots of which are in various locations throughout the frontal lobe, but it also ignores the fact that everything in the brain is connected. Also, it de-emphasizes the role of the limbic system, not to mention the roles of the various neurotransmitters, a discussion of which is beyond the scope of this book.

Secondly, I believe that there really is no such thing as an "Executive Functioning disorder" because there are at least seven different facets of "Executive Functioning," the neurological root of each facet being unique unto itself, even if they all happen to be located in the same general area of the brain (the prefrontal cortex).

And most importantly – parents and teachers, listen up here – ***each and every symptom of NLD is neurologically based***, meaning that none of these are made up to frustrate or annoy you. Those of us with NLD are not "lazy," "stupid," "rude," "crazy," "slackers," "spoiled," or "underachievers." We are doing the best we can, given these limitations that we did not choose for ourselves. These real, physical symptoms have a tremendous impact on our mental, emotional, and spiritual health. How do we deal with all this? Read on – you will find out in Chapter Four.

Chapter Four:
It's All in Your Head – Or is It?

So that's your brain. But, as previously mentioned, there is a great deal of plasticity to your brain. It grows as a result of learning new things, meaning that there are factors other than genetics that affect how your brain works. Most of us did not grow up in complete isolation, or as the only person on a desert island. Instead, we are directly affected by every interaction between ourselves and every other person we encounter. And we are affected indirectly by the interactions between and among everyone around us, such as how our parents relate to each other. When you have NLD, a lot of those interactions can be negative.

NLD and Learned Helplessness

NLD is SO much more than symptoms. It affects the way we think, it may lead to learned helplessness – which is the psychological term for what happens, what you feel when you are perpetually viewed as uncool and so you just stop trying.

Psychologist Martin Seligman coined the term "learned helplessness," which he describes as "the giving-up reaction, the quitting response that follows from the belief that whatever you do doesn't matter."[55]

In their book <u>Learned Helplessness</u>, Christopher Peterson, Steven Maier, and Martin Seligman[56] explain the close parallels between learned helplessness and depression. Of the nineteen points used to diagnose depression (combining those of the symptoms, causes, treatments, and prevention), thirteen match exactly with the facets of learned helplessness, and an additional five are paraphrased equivalents. This means that there is a 95 percent correlation between the diagnoses of learned helplessness and depression.

I feel like I have all these deficits that I am just NOT going to be able to surmount! I feel like everything that I do could easily be interpreted by the world as being less substantive, less creative, less empathic, less intuitive, more pedantic and more automatonic than the average population. I feel like no matter where I go, I'll never be able to connect with anyone (truly).

To others, I seem "clueless" and "incompetent," (their words, not mine). It's not a treatable condition, and I don't think my life can improve far beyond its current state. I can't expect any support from family members, teachers or peers, who would (and have) immediately dismiss it as a stupid excuse.

NLD, Learned Helplessness, and the Classroom

Many classroom teachers are inclined to view us as difficult – not necessarily as troublemakers, but as hard to handle.

We may need to do an assignment more slowly, or differently than others. This gets us labeled as "uncooperative."

We are likely to get lost in the halls, and are told we are "inattentive."

We speak out of turn, and are scolded for being "disruptive."

We inadvertently may upset the process of the academic system by saying what is on our minds, without editing, or by asking too many questions, and are punished for being "rude," "defiant," or "disrespectful."

We don't mean to be uncooperative, inattentive, disruptive, or rude; we are just trying to make sense of what for us is a difficult and often confusing environment. When we not only don't get the answers we are seeking, but also are put down just for asking the questions, we feel more and more helpless. Eventually, we stop asking. Add to this how we get socially shunted aside, are teased, and have few opportunities to participate in the school's "normal" social life. No wonder we may feel depressed, sad, and lonely.

I'll never be normal, so why bother.

Because NLD is so varied in its symptoms and is so hard to diagnose, other students make fun of us. Sometimes the teasing comes from their own frustration, because they cannot understand how to relate to us when we don't know how to relate to them. Our helplessness is reinforced every day. So either we may retreat into a shell, or conversely, try to get attention by showing off, in order to achieve an identity within our peer group.

Everyone in the Special Ed class in elementary school and middle school was teased on the basis of their being part of the "retard class." I know I was beat up in middle school virtually every single day at recess... not because I was really weak, but because I was kind of acting stupid, so to speak. I mean in terms of not knowing how to be cool.

[I experienced] this kind of... social ostracism. It really didn't manifest until high school... I started to become kind of a class clown in middle school, as a result of getting picked on, and I tried to... please to some extent the people who were picking on me. But then in high school... It started out that I would just take certain dares, and... sometimes to get a dollar or something, and sometimes just for laughs. Usually the bet started out sort of benign... like "you think you could..." A typical one might be: "how many packets of McDonald's ketchup do you think you could eat without making yourself sick?"

Special Education Classes: Help or Hindrance?

Special Education (SPED) classes are designed to be only helpful. However, all too often, what ends up happening in many school systems is that all SPED students are lumped together. The teachers have a finite amount of resources to devote to any individual student. In most schools, there simply is not the time or staff necessary to provide us with sufficient opportunities to figure out whether or not we even *could* do the work on our own. Once in SPED, we usually stay there. Meanwhile, our "normal" peers make jokes about the "retard class" (in elementary and middle school at least), and single us out for teasing or bullying. For all the time the SPED teachers expend trying to get us "freaks" from being too unruly, not much is spent on teaching us how to be more "normal."

One would think that at some point, those with dysgraphia actually would be taught how to write more legibly and more quickly, those with ADD would be taught how to pay better attention, and so on. But what teacher has the time, the patience, and the resources to do so? And so, despite the best efforts and intentions of SPED teachers, we LD students still remain dependent on constant assistance from tutors, untimed tests, aides, permission to dictate papers, and so on, at least until we figure out a way out of it all for ourselves, if we are able to do so.

For each student in Special Education, an Individual Education Plan (IEP) is created and reviewed each year. Usually created by a team of SPED and classroom teachers and school administrators, and reviewed by parents and the student, the IEP sets out behavioral, academic, and social goals and objectives for each student to reach.

In theory, the purpose of the IEP and the IEP team meeting is to strive to help the student thrive in the Least Restrictive Environment (LRE), with "mainstreaming" the LD student into the regular classroom as the ultimate goal where appropriate. Unfortunately, all too often the IEP team meeting simply takes measure of how screwed up the LD kid is relative to last year. "How?" you may ask. It's a matter of the way the IEP is worded, which to those of us with NLD, looks something like a CEO writing your New Year's resolutions for you – e.g., "Johnny will improve his gross motor skills by 80%." So, what happens if Johnny falls short of 80% improvement? It doesn't matter who his teachers are, or what exercise he gets at home – it's still worded as though it's his fault. This only serves to indicate how Johnny continues to fall behind and emphasizes his deficits, thereby warranting yet another IEP meeting the following year (and another, and another…).

It is no wonder that learned helplessness is reinforced once an NLD student is assigned to Special Education. Your classmates start teasing you. You may find others in the SPED class who have more recognizable learning disabilities (such as dyslexia or ADD) who tease you too, because even they cannot figure out what your LD is.

SPED students are put down by everyone in school. And there is even a hierarchy within SPED classes, wherein the NLD student is at the bottom. Because even if someone has Down Syndrome or other form of retardation, the others in SPED know what that is and how to deal with it.

There really seems to be a pecking order in school. In the early grades, everyone else puts down the SPED students. They call us "the kids on the short bus." The "in group" of diagnosable LD students might very well put down the un-diagnosable or just plain "weird" children.

...Not only do we end up getting ostracized among our "normal" peers, but there is so much emphasis these days on other, trendier learning disabilities that you could have. I know that these days, ADD is so cool, now autism is up-and-coming and it's very chic to have it, but there doesn't seem to be any real help... if you have NLD.

Nevertheless, by middle school, LD students often put aside our own differences and band together in sympathy. We may become our own social clique, which in turn can make it difficult to interact with any other group.

There really is no definitive answer as to whether or not SPED classes are useful for students with NLD. Like most other facets of living with NLD, it depends. The survey asked, "Were you at any time during your school career in Special Education (SPED) classes? If so, do you feel that these classes were a help or a hindrance and why?" Here is what they said:

No, but I probably should have been, at least for some classes.

Yes. They were a major help. Nobody made fun of you if you had a resource class.

Yes. They were easier usually.

I think that as good as the intentions might have been of whoever thought up the idea of Special Education in the first place, what it really amounts to is just a dumping ground for any kid who doesn't fit the ideal. They were both a help and a hindrance. They were a help to me because they provided me with accommodations.

They were a hindrance to me because I don't think that there was any real effort to have us mainstreamed.

Yes, but only part time – 9ᵗʰ grade and in special speech therapy class. It was a hindrance because I was told to listen instead of read instructions, and I got bored.

They destroyed my self-esteem and did nothing but waste my time.

I felt like I was in a strange position. I didn't need help nearly as much as other kids in a SPED class, but I desperately needed the structure and stress-free atmosphere. No matter where I was, I felt I didn't belong.

NLD and Learned Helplessness at Home

I try. I try really, really hard. But it seems like, no matter what I do, I just screw it up. Last night, I decided I would help out by making pizza for the family's dinner. I fried up some onions, grated the cheese, drained a can of tomatoes, and put all the toppings on the packaged pizza crust and was ready to put it into the oven, when my dad said, "Did you pre-bake the crust?" I hadn't. So I had to scrape everything off and start over. I feel like I can never get it right.

My parents are always urging me to take more initiative. So one winter morning I got up early to surprise them by cleaning the new snowfall off the cars before they had to go to work. Only, there was so much snow, I decided to use a snow shovel to make the work go faster. Instead of being pleased, they were horrified. I realized too late that, apparently, using a metal snow shovel on a new car is not too good for the paint job. My trying to help cost more than a thousand dollars at the body shop.

It should not come as a surprise that, like everything else we learn early in our lives, learned helplessness begins at home. Every human being begins their life helpless. We cannot change the circumstances of our birth, what kind of parents and siblings we have, what socio-economic group we are born into, what parts of our brain and body will develop when, whether we will have peace and tranquility at home, or experience the effects of domestic violence, alcoholism, or our parents' divorce. This reality is true for everyone, not just those with NLD. How our parents react to our NLD is discussed at length in the next chapter.

Like anyone else, we can grasp that certain authority-based rules are the norm ("you have to be at school by 7:45 am," "you are not allowed to drive without a permit"). But while developmentally we are able to comprehend that it is best to obey parents, teachers, and other authorities, often we do not understand *why* these are the rules, and *why* they should apply to us. We want to find out. So we ask questions. And then we ask even more questions. When explanations are not readily forthcoming, or do not make sense, we feel helpless and frustrated.

NLD and Self-Esteem

One of the reasons I wrote this book is that receiving inaccurate information, or sparse information, or no information at all about NLD can and does affect us negatively. It also affects our families, friends, teachers, and everyone else with whom we come in contact regularly. The extent of the effects can be determined only over time.

Unlike more visible learning disabilities, such as AD(H)D or Down Syndrome, NLD is not always immediately apparent. A stranger may wonder about the slow speech or "immature" social skills. A classmate may wonder about the kid in the next row who is always raising her hand to ask questions or who challenges the teacher on every single point. Well-meaning neighbors may ask the high school student, "So what job are you going to get this summer?" All may not understand that these characteristics – the slow speech, the delayed social skills, the questioning, the inability to work at most jobs available to teens – are not character flaws; they are neurological deficits. Others may think of us as lazy, inept, argumentative, or as not trying. All this does is to reinforce how poorly we already may think of ourselves. It underscores how different we are from "normal" neurotypical teens, and makes us feel bad that we can't do what others our age can. In the interviews and surveys, I heard over and over again:

> *I try* really *hard. When you have NLD, your brain has to work a lot harder than most people's. I get tired a lot.*

> *You just can't imagine how hard I am working. You think I'm lazy? Try being inside my head for only one day – you'll see how much energy it takes to be me!*

Time after time, encounter after encounter, we are made to feel "less than" by peers, teachers, even family members – for something that is *not* our fault. The longer we and those around us lack clear, accurate information on what NLD is and how to deal with it, the longer the same prejudices and stereotypes will continue. Enough such encounters, unless counterbalanced by a great number of successes, easily can lead to learned helplessness and even to depression.

Is it any surprise, then, that many of us, especially when we are young, have such low self-esteem? From adults, who often don't understand us, we are told we are "troublemakers," "rude" or "stupid" at worst, and "not trying hard enough" or "underachievers" at best. From the adults who do understand, we may hear that our work needs to be edited or supervised, due to our lack of understanding of social norms (such as what is "acceptable" language in an academic paper). It may be well-intentioned help, but it can feel like censorship. From classmates who don't understand NLD, we are called "retards," or "losers," and are viewed as "uncool." Moreover, peers who are mature enough to understand or at least respect our differences are few and far between, and even then, they don't totally "get" us:

> *There was the time in 10th grade when I got a "D" in sculpture because I just couldn't make anything. And, like, I couldn't form the stuff I was working with at the time into what I wanted…and of course, everybody was like, "You got a 'D' in sculpture?!" 'cause it's an easy class.*

So now what? Are we sunk? Is there any hope? Can you have a successful life with NLD? "It depends," say the dozens of people who were interviewed or who responded to the online survey.

While there is no denying that the neurological deficits associated with NLD are real, they are not the source of the most difficult challenges for NLDers. Those come from:

1. how you are perceived by and treated by others, and

2. how you feel about that and consequently, how you perceive yourself.

These two factors are iterative. That means that one leads to the other, which feeds on the other, in a kind of never-ending feedback loop. When you are perceived as clumsy, disorganized and a screw-up, over time you start to think about yourself that way. Then you tend to live up to (or down to) others' expectations of you.

If you treat yourself with respect, others treat you better.

Helplessness and Hopefulness

The nature of NLD makes it difficult to *unlearn* helplessness. However, teasing or criticism from one's peers, at least in the pre-adolescent years, is not a sentence of doom, nor a permanent marker for hopelessness in and of itself. Also, with respect to teasing and learned helplessness, remember that these events apply mostly to childhood and early adolescence. As we get older, friends and peers tend to be more understanding. Plus both we and our friends more fully grasp the concepts of diversity, disability, and differences as we all mature.

[The one person who I think really understands my condition would be] my friend Dan who I became friends with starting in 6th grade. He's really become a confidante that I can always rely on. I've explained a lot more about the NLD since [we met]. But I think he's probably one of the most reliable friends I have.

Given our negative early experiences, one might think that we feel helpless or hopeless all or most of the time. But the best news is that these feelings can and do improve for most of us as we get older. When asked: "Do you feel helpless or hopeless regarding your condition? Why or why not?" the replies were:

> *Very hopeless. I've been in the hospital for most of 9 months ... Tried most every antidepressant (including MAOI) and mood stabilizer. Even electroshock therapy failed. I'm hospitalized now. (female, 18)*

> *Yes. It's disabling and lonely. (male, 18)*

> *Yes. I'm afraid of the future. (male, 18)*

> *Yes. I'm afraid to ask people for things. (female, 18)*

> *Sometimes I do because I feel that people don't understand how hard it is to meet people. (female, 20)*

> *I do on occasion. Sometimes I simply cannot visualize myself being successful or even independent because of the various aspects and global impact of my disability. Then again, I am not that good at visualizing or foresight so perhaps that is understandable. (male, 20)*

> *I often feel helpless when I have trouble doing basic everyday tasks. When the simplest tasks are impossible for me and no one understands, it makes me feel isolated and worthless. (female, age 21).*

> *Yes. I am in a cycle of not getting work done because it is too daunting a task. (female, 22)*

> *Yes, because I know certain things, such as my spatial deficit and difficulty with reading social cues, will always be difficult for me no matter how hard I work. (female, 23)*

> *Yes. I work so damn hard, all the time, and I still don't have friends. I get tired of trying so hard. I get tired of people saying, "If only you did X or Y, then you wouldn't have this problem," or "If only your parents raised you differently, then you'd be normal." I'm not normal, and I get tired of being reminded of that all the time. It seems like everybody else gets ahead and I'm still stuck behind. I wonder if anybody would notice if I dropped off the planet. (female, 23)*

I used to [feel hopeless], but when I went to college I could see what burnouts some of the other kids were, and that they were taking drugs or drinking, or worrying about their fancy clothes and their boyfriends and I could see that even with NLD my life wasn't so bad in comparison. (female, 25)

Sometimes because I get discouraged during school when I had a tough time with subjects – Algebra II, and sentence diagramming in English. (female, 25)

Yes, sometimes, because it prevents me from getting a job, and I don't really have that much of a clue about dating. (male, 26)

Not anymore. I get frustrated with lack of services, though. (female, 27)

I feel both helpless and hopeless on a regular basis. I am 27 years old, I have never been out on a date, and I have no idea even how to start on romantic relationships. I live with my parents and got fired from my first job out of college. (female, 27)

I used to, but I really don't anymore. I think I am finally starting to get the fact that I am fine just the way I am and if other people don't like it, that's their problem. I just stay clear of those kinds of negative people. (male, 30)

Yes, but only when dealing with my son's school and IEP team (female, 31)

From listening to these young adults, it seems that most – but not all – people with NLD become more positive, self-reliant and resilient over time. What is important to note is that of those who reported feeling helpless and/or hopeless, the nature of these feelings changed over time. What first manifested as desperation, fear, and depression, later was just frustration – either at the persistent symptoms or at the lack of accommodations and understanding.

This finding may indicate that whereas teens with NLD may view their whole *life* as futile, those who are some 10 years older tend to be more pragmatic. We can separate our life from our symptomatic difficulties, frustrating though they might be.

When asked, "Do you ever feel sorry for yourself? Why or why not?" the younger respondents' replies reflected their negative feelings, but the replies generally became more positive the older the respondent.

>*Yes. I have not had one week un-depressed in 2 ½ years. (female, 18)*

>*Yes. I lost my purse the other day. I had to ask my friend to come to the police with me to pick it up once I learned they had it. I should have been able to do that on my own. (female, 18)*

>*Yes. People can be mean. (male, 19)*

>*On occasion, but I never let others know about it. I keep it all in. I don't feel justified in complaining to others. Plus, I don't like to talk about my condition at all. (male, 20)*

>*Sometimes, because I feel I don't have many friends and I don't go out much. I see everyone go out and I get jealous. (female, 20)*

>*Yes. I see all these profiles on Facebook, and I just notice how full everybody else's lives seem. Everybody else's except mine. I have this really funny Facebook profile, but I only have one picture up there. I have no pictures with friends. I have no friends. Just acquaintances. It seems like it's never going to end. (male, 20)*

>*Regrettably, I do catch myself feeling sorry for myself. These feelings tend to arise when I'm having extreme difficulty with a task and I know the problem could be easily solved or prevented altogether if I had the appropriate support. However, because people don't understand NLD there doesn't seem to be much support or help available. (female, 21)*

>*No, I don't feel sorry for myself. Failure simply causes me to hate myself. It's a sign that I can't accomplish the simplest of tasks, and that the road ahead will simply be more of the same. (male, 21)*

>*Yes and no. On the one hand, I know that I am wealthy compared to most of the world. I have a wonderful mother and people in my life who care about me. I have good food and a warm bed. But, one of the things necessary for human happiness (really, I read it somewhere) is community and friendship. I don't have that. It seems ridiculous to ask for more than I have, but I just want some normal rewards for my*

hard work. I want friends, and I don't think that's too much to ask, but apparently it is. (female, 23)

> *No, not at all. (female, 23)*

> *I used to feel sorry for myself quite often, but these days I realize I can have a life I can be happy with in my life with NLD. Even though NLD can make life hard sometimes, I have a lot to be thankful for. (female, 23)*

> *Just once in a while. I wish I could drive. I wish I had a boyfriend. (female, 25)*

> *Yes. Doesn't everyone? (male, 26)*

> *Not anymore. (female, 27)*

> *Yes, although I am better at snapping out of it than I used to be. (female, 27)*

> *Only a little bit. Because of my NLD and not-so-good concentration, I figured it was not a good idea for me to drive, but I live in a large city, so there is plenty of public transportation. (male, 30)*

> *Why should I? I'm the good one! (female, age 31)*

Here, again, we can see a trend in the answers showing that, as NLDers get older, we become less sorry for ourselves, and that when we do, it manifests far less as desperation and depression, and more as simply philosophical introspection.

So what can we – and those around us – do to ensure that we continue to have the very best chance to build on our successes and to meet the challenges that may come our way? In the next chapters, we will look at how parents can help, what teachers can do, and the actual strategies and techniques that have helped us, and which you can use to help yourself.

A note to the teen reader: Chapter Five is meant to be read by parents and teachers, so the "you" in that chapter means them, not you. But I hope you read it anyway and discuss it with your own parents and teachers.

Chapter Five:
Talking to Parents and Teachers About NLD

It is crucial for parents and teachers to know exactly what is wrong, and more often, what is right, with their child or student. It is even more crucial for the NLD student to know exactly what is "wrong" and "right" with him or herself.

Having NLD affects not only the individual, but the whole family as well. A teen with NLD who is angry or confused can upset the whole family dynamic, whereas one who is calm and happy can affect the family for the better.

One way to keep the peace is to make sure that the household runs smoothly, in an orderly fashion, and with as little disruption as possible. Some of the ways we have found that work well follow.

- Tell your teen exactly what his or her household responsibilities and chores are, when he or she needs to do them, and critically important – what constitutes a good job!

I'm very literal, and logical... I need a lot of things explained to me very, very, very explicitly ...I think that kind of annoys some of the people I live with ... There have been many times while I was growing up, if my mom said to me "do the dishes," I do just that: I empty the dishwasher, load it again, and leave. And she might get upset with me, because it was "ever-so-obvious" that I had to not only empty and load it, but also clean out the sink and clean up the counters, and then rinse out the sponge. As if that were somehow implied.

We find it really, really helps to have a printed list posted somewhere where your teen can see it.

If it's not written down, it's not gonna happen!

- Post a written meal plan for the week on the refrigerator. This helps in two ways: one, if your teen knows what is planned for dinner, he or she is less likely to snack on one of the main dinner ingredients. And two, if your teen is responsible for doing some of the meal preparation and cooking for the family, he or she then knows exactly what's for dinner, without having to plan it.

Cooking is easy and fun – but deciding what *to make for dinner is just about impossible!*

- Household rules concerning things like homework time and bedtime; limits on TV, radio, video games, Internet, Facebook time, and cell phone use should be discussed, explained logically, and probably written down and posted somewhere.
- Teens should be included in family discussions, and where appropriate, their opinions should be taken into consideration in major family decisions.

By the time we are in high school, we should get to help decide where we go on our summer vacation. I am so tired of my parents treating me like a baby and saying, "We're going to the beach again" when my best friend's family lives in our old hometown and I really would much rather spend some time with him.

It was really horrible when my collie Sheila broke her leg. My parents wanted to take her to the vet to put her down, but I wanted the vet to try to do surgery first. I mean, we got her when I was in kindergarten and she was pretty much my best friend. Then I found out it was going to cost more than $3000 to do the surgery, and it might not even work that well. My parents didn't want to pay that much money for an old dog. I said I would use my college fund and they finally said I could. But the vet told me that Sheila really wouldn't ever recover, and that it was better for her not to have to suffer. But after a couple of days of watching Sheila limp around all groggy from painkillers, I finally had to agree that she should be put to sleep.

I can understand that my parents sometimes have to make major decisions for the family. When it was time to paint the house, I helped choose the colors for the family room and kitchen, and I had complete control over the colors for my new room.

Remember That We Don't Like Change

Because most NLDers do not adapt easily or happily to change, one of the most helpful things parents can do to make family life easier is to clearly explain in advance, whenever possible, any changes in routine or family life that may be imminent.

For example, remember the story in Chapter Three about the teen who was so upset when his parents replaced the track lighting in the living room that he actually broke down and cried? What could his parents have done to help avoid that? The conversation could go something like this:

"Son, we are going to make some changes in our living room next week, and we want to tell you why. Just like clothes go in and out of fashion, so do lighting fixtures. In the early 1980s, when you were born, the track lighting that we now have was very stylish. But now, 25 years later, it looks dated and we want to replace it with more modern recessed lighting. Plus, the track lights make the room very hot in the summer, as you know.

"So we have picked out some new fixtures. Here's a brochure that shows what they will look like. Mr. Johnson, the electrician, will be coming over when you get home from school next Tuesday. He will take out the old lights and install the new ones for us.

"We know that these lights have been here ever since you can remember, and that this change will be upsetting for you. But these are our reasons and we hope that soon, you will enjoy our attractive new lights too."

What are the important elements of this little speech?

- Inform your teen ahead of time so he or she can prepare intellectually for the change.

- Logically explain the need for the change (in this case, there are two reasons).

- Either inform him/her that either you already have made a final decision (as in this case) or that his/her input will be welcomed, if appropriate.

- Acknowledge that he or she feels upset about the change, and

- Reassure him/her that he or she probably will be happy with the new results in a short time.

My parents taught me that in our house we follow the Golden Rule: "The one who has the gold makes the rules!" I didn't understand this when I was younger, until they explained that "gold" meant "money" and that the one who is putting up the money for something gets to decide what to buy.

"Because I Said So" – NOT!

The worst thing parents can tell a NLD teen is: "because I said so." That just drives us crazy with frustration. We are not *being defiant. We really need a logical reason for what you are asking us to do. Honestly.*

Parents, should you ever think of using the line "…because I said so" with your NLD teen, *don't*. Maybe you read a child development book written for "normal" neurotypical children, which says that children will grasp the idea that parents have a right to say "because I said so" by virtue of their position of authority and responsibility in the family. The child or teen, being a child and not an adult, needs to learn that when a parent speaks, he or she must obey.

And maybe that is true for a neurotypical child or teen. But because of the way our brains are wired, we will not respect you based solely on your authority (at least not until we reach our mid-twenties to early thirties, and by then we will no longer need your daily guidance).

NLDers either have no idea what the "because I said so" line means, or we think we know exactly what it means: "you feel the need to use your authority to coerce us into doing what you want." In either case, we can't conceive of why doing something "because you said so" is in any way important or significant *to us*. Instead, we will look at you, mystified, wondering why you would say something so irrational, and also wonder why you are wasting your time or ours.

Here is a helpful hint. If it is absolutely necessary that you must use the "because I said so" line on your NLD teen, it would be a good idea to first explain what "because I said so" actually means. Better yet, to save you both the time and energy, before you tell us to do the chore or task in question, tell us first that there will be a break in the ordinary, daily schedule that necessitates doing that particular chore or task.

An example might be: "I get really upset and frankly, kind of nauseated, when I look at your messy room. I know you don't want me to go in there and barf on your books and CDs – so go clean it up!"

Or another: "Grandma and Grandpa are coming over, and I want your room to look clean to please them. Because they are my parents, it makes me feel bad when they think I'm not an effective parent to you." Contrast these two reasons with: "Clean your room (because I said so)."

Another example is: "It's going to rain tonight, so you need to mow the lawn today instead of tomorrow, when the grass will be too wet to cut," as opposed to just, "Mow the lawn now (because I said so)."

Yes, we know it takes more of your time to explain things, but think of all the time you'll save by not having to engage in incessant arguing!

Most parents try to be helpful if they can, but wind up just as frustrated or confused as we are, until they learn more about NLD.

> *I also wish my parents had known about my NLD when I was younger. Since learning about the diagnosis they have been my biggest advocates, but when I was younger they attributed NLD-related issues to lack of effort.*

Probably the single most important thing parents can do is *to learn more about NLD* (so thanks for reading this book).

Well, sometimes my father is a little surprised at…some of the things I can't do, but it's nothing major. There's not been anything dramatic like that.

   When my parents first found out that there was a vague diagnosis and I sort of explained to them what it was, they – I can remember this so clearly – we were in the car, and I don't remember where we were going, but the two of them were fighting: "It's my fault!" "It's my fault!" kind of thing. It's really kind of funny. And my dad was particularly hard on himself, so I gave him an example of something that someone with NLD might do that definitely would not have come from him…

But the message you give your NLD teen may not be as benign or supportive as this story. One recurrent theme in a family in which one child has some kind of "problem" (certainly not exclusive to families with an NLDer), is that one parent may be (mostly) supportive and understanding, while the other parent is in complete denial that there even is a problem.

   Well, my mom is supportive, but she wants me to continue to take – I'm pretty sure it was [name of medication] – but I'm pretty sure it has barely any effect, I mean, I burn too much. So I don't want to take it anymore. So that's the only thing we disagree on. The strange thing is, it's also an anti-depressant, but &#$% that. My dad, on the other hand, doesn't really want me to… never wanted to accept that I had NLD. My dad is willing to help me any way he can, but if… uh, if anything new… any new kind of disability crops up, he doesn't want to accept it. Like, I could have Asperger's Syndrome, but he's decided that's an umbrella term that doesn't mean anything, and so I don't have it. So that's my dad's reaction to be supportive, but wanting to deny, you know.

And to their teen, parents either respond with: "We're getting you help, getting you into special education classes," or "We're getting you a therapist," or sometimes, even worse: "What's *wrong* with you? Why can't you just behave yourself?"

It's really hard sometimes, when you have NLD and even your own family doesn't get it. My father for example, yells at me all the time to try harder. Once he sent an email which said, "My goal is to have [you] free of the need for LD status…the time is good for [you] to move to be fully normalized (sic)." As if!

When it comes to siblings and extended family members, they also may not understand much about NLD.

I have a half-sister who is much older than I am, and I don't think she knows. Beyond my parents, nobody really knows because it was never really important until last year when I actually had a name for something.

My brother really doesn't get it. He just gets embarrassed when I do socially awkward things at school. But, you know, he will still stick up for me if the other kids tease me. It really helps to know he loves me, even if he doesn't always understand that I can't help it.

Some siblings know a little about NLD, but may "wish it away:"

Well, I mean, I really don't want to talk about it… but the immediate family member who upsets me the most though is my sister, who is not in denial that I have a problem, but she doesn't want me to confront my father about the fact that there is something wrong with me that cannot be fixed. She doesn't want me to confront him because she doesn't want to cause trouble. And because she's my sister, that really troubles me. I mean I wouldn't just go out and tell her, "there's only one way that this can be resolved, and that's for me to tell him either to accept me or go take a hike." But I really just don't like the fact that usually she takes no side at all, and if she takes a side, it's always his.

But siblings also can be our best friends and champions:

> *My brother is two years older than me, and he actually punched a kid who was teasing me in the cafeteria. I was sad 'cause he got in trouble with the principal, but you know – they stopped teasing me!*
>
> *My sister is really the one person I can always count on to help and to listen.*

What We Want Our Parents to Know

Parents, whether or not you understood the information in Chapter Three about neural connections and language is not as important as *understanding that we do not argue with you merely to drive you crazy*. Rather, it is because we are really confused by the myriad of what are to us illogical rules and inconsistencies and to which we are expected to conform.

> *[I wish my parents had known] that I wasn't being difficult on purpose.*
>
> *I wish they had known (I wish my father could get this pounded into his thick head now, actually, as he still thinks I'm making it up) that I wasn't having meltdowns on purpose, and that I really "couldn't" eat the food on my plate due to sensory sensitivities. But, I'm also glad that they didn't know about my NLD, because they pushed me further than I ever would have gotten if they had known about my diagnosis earlier.*
>
> *I do believe it might have been helpful for my parents to have kept more of an open dialogue about my NLD than they had.*
>
> *[I wish my parents had known] that I was not a lazy ass.*

Our NLD is real and it is not going away. Having NLD is not something we can change about ourselves, though we can make accommodations and compensations for it. In other words, if there is some aspect of NLD in which we improve over time, then great. Otherwise, we hope you can learn to live with it. We certainly have to.

One thing I wish my father knew is that this is me, and you can't just wish it away. The thing I wish my mother had known is that I had NLD, and that means I would be living at home a lot longer than she'd planned for when she had me.

I don't think my parents knew anything about learning disabilities. I think schools and teachers need to undergo more training in LD so they are better able to identify problems in students and to refer their families to appropriate professionals.

I wish my father would understand that I am not *making this up. My mother is pretty good about getting it, and helps me any way she can.*

That I had it, and home and school would have not been so frustrating. If my parents knew I had a different learning style, they could have taught me things in a different way, so it wouldn't have been so frustrating for everyone.

Because our NLD is here to stay, it is imperative that you, the parent, do your best to understand us and NLD. But for heaven's sake, *don't baby us.*

When I first got to high school and we had just found out I had NLD, my mom wanted to hand out these little pamphlets she had printed up to all my teachers, explaining NLD and how they could help me. This was SO incredibly embarrassing. I didn't want to hurt her feelings, so I just chucked them all in the waste basket the minute I got to school.

Instead, help us **build on our strengths**:

I wish they had pushed me to get involved in the community more.

[I wish my parents had known] how smart I was.

[I wish my parents had known] that maybe we could've found a different way to do my physical therapy, because touching my left leg felt really uncomfortable when I was younger; and I would laugh (it was like tickling, but not quite), and my mom would laugh.

[I wish my parents had known] that I just can't do everything everyone else can.

And please help us to understand the nuances of things that may seem obvious to others our age. In addition to not understanding the rules of social interaction, unlike most kids, teens with NLD often do not absorb the norms of our culture except through direct experience. This is why we often need a parent or other adult to "interpret" the rules for us.

One day when I was fifteen and had just come home from school, the little boy next door rang the bell. He and his friend wanted to come in and play with our cat, as he and his little sister often did. "Sure," I told him, and let them in and went back downstairs where I was doing my homework. I forgot all about them, until about an hour later when the doorbell rang. It was the police. Apparently, he didn't tell his mom that they were going to our house. When the friend's mother came to pick up her son, and the boys couldn't be found, she got hysterical. They called the police. Even though our neighbor told her I was a nice guy, when the lady saw that her five-year-old son had been in the house with a teenager, she went ballistic, and wanted to have me arrested. The police asked me a lot of questions, and then called my mother home from work. My mother had to explain to me that there were bad guys who sometimes hurt little boys. That never would have crossed my mind when I was fifteen. I was so shocked and sad. I would never hurt anyone.

Fortunately, some of our parents actually get it and understand how to help:

I think they did know [what to do to help] and now that I'm older, it is out of their hands completely.

The benefit of being the child of a special education director is that you're immediately subjected to a battery of tests at the first sign of a learning disability. I think they knew everything they needed to know about [having NLD].

As was already discussed in Chapter Three, I think the one most critically important fact for parents to keep in mind is the finding that both the social skills and Executive Functioning skills of a person with NLD typically make us act and react as would a neurotypical person about 75% of their chronological age. That is, an 18-year-old with NLD may not be ready to leave home to go to college, but may be just about ready for summer camp.

> *I failed royally at the first college I went to, so the next term, my folks sent me to a college specifically for kids with learning disabilities. Despite the fact that I still failed virtually every class I took, at least I was having a really good time. I was having fun wasting my life away, downloading and playing NES, SNES, and Genesis ROMs on my computer, and subsequently having seizures from playing them nonstop, even though I have photo-sensitive epilepsy, and knew I wasn't supposed to be gaming. Because there were no restrictions on what you could eat or drink, every day, I always got bacon and eggs for breakfast; every night when I went down to the game room, I always ordered buffalo wings and either jalapeño poppers or mozzarella sticks; and I averaged about 5-6 12 oz. glasses of Coke a day. When I first showed up there in the summer of 2000, I weighed 190 lb., but when I was asked to leave in May 2002, I weighed 285 lb. But I was having fun, wasn't I? Every week or so, there was a van to take us to the local cinema, and once a semester, there was some kind of field trip (the best was to the local Six Flags). But despite all of this, I hated my life. I was a fat tub of lard, I had no chance in hell of getting a girlfriend, I was failing most of my classes, I missed my family, and anything resembling the religious services I used to attend at home was completely inaccessible to me. But, at least having to survive some of my roommates helped me improve my social skills!*

There are so many questions about NLD and the family for which we simply don't have any answers yet.

What We Want Therapists and Guidance Counselors to Know

> *You might understand the clinical aspects of NLD but you can't possibly know what it's like to live with it.*

Sometimes, when parents don't have answers to these questions or others, you might turn to therapists or to school guidance counselors as a resource, or to seek help for your teen with NLD. We understand that you are trying to be helpful, and we are not saying that all therapy is futile. However, a lot of us have had negative experiences with therapy, and have very strong negative feelings about it.

Respondents who mentioned being in therapy either disliked or mistrusted (or both) at least one or more past therapists. Looking back, we wish our therapists were more helpful:

> *I couldn't deal with somebody who was bad at being understanding, who was just not a good psychologist... this guy tried to placate kids with teddy bears and shit. But he didn't try to make kids feel at ease... you gotta choose somebody who's going to make an NLD student feel at ease. Because I was emotionally tough, you know – I don't know if emotional sensitivity is part of the NLD, or a difficulty dealing with emotions, not necessarily sensitivity. But whatever, there should be a psychologist that deals with that...*
>
> *In all the so-called expertise, advancing through their psychology major and degrees, they don't have that much actual experience with either having a learning disability themselves, or living with someone with a learning disability, or even having a large number of LD students... They really should know that a LOT of the classical training that they teach you in child development is absolutely not useful at all if you're a NLD student, especially the Piaget.*
>
> *[Therapists should] not be so excessively assuming, like, someone assuming "oh, you just had a bad childhood" or that it's some psychological defense mechanism, or anything like that.*
>
> *Well, I've never been really honest with my... specialists. Always like... I am being honest with you [the interviewer], but... when I was a kid, it just didn't seem worth the effort to tell these people the real truth.*

The survey asked: "If you could tell therapists one thing about NLD, what would that be? The respondents were not shy about speaking their minds:

> *[NLD] exists, please look for it.*
>
> *Please recognize this disorder and provide help to those that need it. If NLD was more widely accepted and well known, my life would be a lot easier.*
>
> *If everything appears to be all right, that doesn't mean that it is. As a student with NLD, I am very good at hiding how I feel. I don't think that is a choice.*
>
> *I'm not sure... probably that they were looking at my disability from the wrong angle, I guess.*
>
> *Please speak to me directly and say what you feel.*
>
> *Create small steps in a learning process and repeat these steps over and over again until the person gets it. Then move on to a following step.*
>
> *I need more time with you. I need your flexibility. I need you to take the extra steps I cannot see, ask the questions I do not know to ask ... I need you to lead.*
>
> *Just because I can do something in the testing room, it does not mean that I can apply that skill in real life.*
>
> *They can't change me.*
>
> *Just because we're not developing according to the normal theories of development does not mean that there is anything wrong with us. Also, that before you go labeling, you really have to stop and consider: is there such a thing as a "normal" brain or an "ideal" brain?*
>
> *Stop theorizing all over me. I am a person, not a case in a textbook. Just because you had another patient some time ago with NLD doesn't make me like them.*

Preparing Your NLD Teen for the Upper Grades

With respect to preparing a teen with NLD for middle school, when the work starts to get more difficult and papers are required, parents have a big job. If they hear from the school that their child is acting out or is being disruptive in school, and/or is a general nuisance to teach, they genuinely may be confused about what, exactly, the problem might be, thinking, "Our child seems nice to us. Now he or she is doing poorly in school. Where did we go wrong?"

What parents need to understand is that whereas the early grades were "easy," once you add in the requirements of writing papers, having to change teachers and classrooms every hour, and meeting up with a whole new group of kids, among other challenges, all of which require skills in which we are not too adept, we may just collapse under the pressure.

> *... if your academic career is like a race, then the LD student is starting out*
> *100 feet behind everyone else.*

We may feel especially sad and confused because we started our academic careers with such promise. In addition to being very bright, we often have an extensive vocabulary and command of the written language at a very early age. We may have been misunderstood in the earlier grades, but the consequences were less severe, and what in others might be strengths can actually get us into trouble as we proceed up through the grades.

> *In third grade, I did a report on Canyon de Chelly. I got the report back with a*
> *C+, and a comment: "Next time, put it in your own words." I was astounded! It was a*
> *great report. No one had helped me at all, not even with the spelling. It was in my*
> *own words. Because I wasn't yet diagnosed, the teacher didn't understand the*
> *disparity between my verbal IQ and performance IQ. She assumed I had plagiarized*
> *the work.*

> *I really disliked language classes in elementary school. For one thing, I*
> *already knew most of the vocabulary words, and I had been reading since I was three.*
> *The classes were counterproductive. You got marked down, not only for being*
> *loquacious, but also for knowing what "loquacious" means.*

So many of us started out as one of the "smart kids," and then progressively fell further and further behind. It's not your fault. It's probably not your teachers' fault, either, but that of the teaching *methods*. Rote memorization of arithmetic tables and simple vocabulary (which you probably already know), in-class journal writing (which is torture) and assigned essays, book reports, and longer term papers are the bane of students with NLD.

> *I basically know going in I will not pass. I just pray I completed enough home and extra credit to pass. Scantrons are the worst invention ever made.*

With these kinds of assignments, you may start to "show your true colors" with respect to your organizational deficiencies. Many of us just shut down and stop trying. Our teachers and parents think we are just being stubborn. What they need to know is: it's not that we *won't* do these assignments; we *can't*. Many of us with NLD also are perfectionists: we will not do an assignment unless we can do it right.

> *It took me a very long time – I think I was already in college – before I finally understood that you do not just sit down and start with one perfect sentence, and then follow that with several more perfect sentences, paragraphs and pages. Even the best writers do draft after draft, throwing away the crappy stuff, and polishing their words til they get it right. And even then, they often aren't completely happy with the finished work. I never understood how you could turn in a piece that wasn't perfect. But even professional writers just do the best they can. That's what editors are for!*

We may have wonderful ideas, but need help in translating them to paper or other media:

> *Art was extremely painful. I have memories of being in the first grade and leaving completely blank a booklet that was supposed to be drawn in. I flat out refused to draw. One project I did in school was make an "art-exterminator" out of clay which would do all of my art assignments for me. My mother had to make the entire thing for me but the idea was mine.*

Social Interaction in School

Not understanding the rules of social interaction in school is a serious detriment to those of us with NLD. When we were younger, our parents, older siblings, and teachers probably watched out for us, and prevented us from making total fools of ourselves. Now that we are older, we have to learn to do this for ourselves. It really can be difficult when we don't "get" the unwritten rules our peers somehow seem to intuit. In school or in social interactions, we may speak out of turn, ask questions that others consider inappropriate, and generally disrupt the learning process, even though we do not intend to be rude or disobedient.

In fourth grade, our class took a field trip to Orchard House in Concord – the home of the Alcotts and the place where Louisa May wrote Little Women. We were greeted at the door by a gentle older woman in 19th century dress, who welcomed us by saying, 'Hello children. I am Marmee, Louisa May's mother. I am so glad you could visit our home.' I knew she wasn't telling the truth. Marmee lived in the 1800s and this was 1990. As she spoke, I grew more and more uncomfortable and confused. I knew that lying is wrong. And she was definitely not telling the truth. I was angry, I didn't know why someone was lying to me, not just about her name, but also about the fact that she could pretend to be something she wasn't. Finally, I couldn't take it anymore, and much to the chagrin of my class and teacher, I decided it was time to reveal the truth. "You're not the real Marmee!" I shouted, and my teacher led me out of the room. I was so angry that I was being censured for telling the truth. Truth is very important to me. I felt betrayed.

What could the teacher have done ahead of time to prevent this situation? She could have said, "When we go on the field trip tomorrow, there will be an actress who will be playing the part of Marmee. As part of her acting role, she may even say she is Marmee, so don't let it throw you. She isn't lying, she is acting, and that is OK." The problem is, though, that unless we were in a very small class, and the teacher knew us very well, she probably couldn't have anticipated this in advance.

We know you may be frustrated teaching us. But please don't ever resort to physical tactics, or to shunting us off to guidance counselors because you don't know what else to do. There usually is another way.

> *I started to zone out, especially during math and physics classes, and the teacher took me by the head and asked me to pay attention. (Gestures the teacher shaking him.) Well, not like shook me or anything, just held me by the head (laughs). Uh... I... ya know, I felt, I felt like it was a loss of control, and I sort of liked that teacher, except for when he was a jerk....*
>
> *Hello! (to teacher) It's YOU who needs to be guidance counseled, not me. Just because YOU don't get how I learn, doesn't me there is anything wrong with me.*

So how *can* teachers help the student with NLD? The survey asked: "If you could tell your grade school (K-12) teachers one thing they should know about NLD, what would that be?" The respondents had plenty to say.

What We Want Our Teachers to Know

> *[Teachers] should not assume that we're deliberately being stubborn or socially clumsy, or any way someone could negatively perceive us... when somebody has these kinds of issues, it's not something deliberate... teachers should not whip through explanations of topics too fast. And often, students with learning disabilities take a longer time to really absorb the information, and if she just whips through it, the student may not pick up on something highly crucial.*
>
> *I have never really had any teachers who I got very close to.*

We ARE working hard!
> *Do not tell me, "you need to try harder."*
>
> *Show compassion.*

You have no idea how hard my brain was working. You kept telling me I wasn't trying but I was, I really was!

I'm not lazy, this is just who I am. I need all the help I can get.

NLD people work really, really hard, even if you can't see it!!!

Be patient. Please, for the love of God, be patient with me. Also, never ever give me another journal assignment again. Those are torture.

Forget all your theories. Please teach us using methods that will help us learn.
Teach me verbally!

Create ways to talk about the information being presented. In math classes, have the students talk out the reasons for completing each step.

Be very straightforward with all that you tell and ask students with NLD.

That I need things said verbally. If things aren't said verbally, I will not understand.

If a child is rude, they do not mean to be. Please do not punish them. Also, please teach kids with NLD that it is OKAY to tattle. I'm 23, and I still have nightmares about middle and high school because I thought it was wrong to rat on the bullies.

Please make time to learn more about NLD.
You really "can" get As in advanced reading and Cs in slow math, and it's not because of laziness.

I don't care how smart you think I am. I am doing the best I can.

Get training and be honest with parents about the fact that you are not medical professionals, your goal is to educate, not treat, these conditions.

Don't jump to conclusions about students and their abilities, and for God's sake, get over yourselves.

In grades K-6 watch [for the signs of NLD]: [poor] handwriting, reading beyond grade level. In grades 7-12, [watch for] learning style.

[In terms of] test taking, present tests that are similar to the homework so we know what to expect.

Give me less work.

If I show you that I can do one math problem, I don't need to do 100 a night. Five maybe, but not 100. You can't imagine how long this takes me.

Just because I am not taking notes does not mean I don't hear what you are saying.

We need and deserve your respect. We may feel that we don't want to even bother trying in classrooms with teachers who don't understand us and who see us as incompetent.

Well, they should have known that... well all right... it depends on which teacher, I guess. The teachers that were unprepared to be teachers, the ones that are in public schools now, should know that if they weren't prepared for an NLD student, they shouldn't even try, because they're just not going to do a good job. And with teachers who actually care, and who actually have looked into what an NLD student needs, they should know that – usually I have wanted to make an effort, thought it might not seem like it. When a teacher studies what NLD is, that's different from actually encountering a student or a person with NLD.

Our frustration may be aimed not at the teachers, but more at the administration:

(Smiles) I'm not going to need sculpture in my life. I would like it in my life, but if it's not there, then that's fine. I don't need to have this... art in my diploma. It's not something that is necessary for people coming from your school to have. It's not something anybody's going to look for... up there, like, really going over my education with a fine tooth comb, they're not gonna look and say, "Oh, no! This school doesn't have any kind of Art requirements. We don't know if there's any kind of Art in his history. We can't hire him." It's just, it's just pointless.

We don't just have a learning disability – we are individuals too!

[We] can do anything normal kids can do, even if it takes longer, and [you need] to recognize the different learning style. Allow us to take classes that we are motivated to take, like taking a foreign language.

Teachers and administrators: don't assume that we are all bad in math, or good in English just because that's what you've read in the NLD literature. We are as varied as any other students in the classes we like and dislike, and in which we do well or poorly. The survey asked: "Was there a class in grade school that was a total waste of time?" We said:

Religion.

Math (I didn't get it), arts and PE (I couldn't do it.)

Gym class.

Algebra. Latin.

Math, gym.

Chorus. I don't think I can despise chorus enough.

Gym, social studies, language.

Maybe "family life" class in middle school. (A lot of people without disabilities would probably agree with me, though ;-)).

Any class that didn't verbalize the curriculum.

Gym. I hated it and it hated me right back. It was pure torture. Also, I couldn't learn languages, so I don't know why my parents had me switch them – I flunked Spanish as badly as I flunked Latin.

Nothing a waste of time, difficulty in gym class and art class.

Algebra and Latin.

And, on a more positive note:

Not really. I was interested in learning, even when I wasn't too good at it.

You Absolutely Have the Ability to Change Our Lives for the Better!

In an ideal world, where funding for education is limitless and all teachers are enlightened enough to embrace the concept of many kinds of learners with many kinds of learning styles, and where every single public school student actually had an Individual Education Plan that works (the most democratic approach to school) there would be no learning disabilities, only, perhaps, teaching disabilities. But in our less-than-perfect system of public education, what can one teacher do?

The things we struggle with are real, and our struggles are often unnoticed. Look for the signs, because the entire direction of a child's life can be changed if the appropriate interventions are made.

A teacher who takes the time to notice, who makes the time to help, can have long-lasting, life-changing effects. The survey asked: "Have you had any teachers who changed your life for the better? If so, please tell us about one." The respondents were enthusiastic about the good, caring teachers they had:

Yes, despite not knowing about my NLD, I had teachers who saw my potential and spent extra time helping me grow as a student and person. I appreciate that.

My Dutch [language] teacher in high school had personal conversations with me and kept on telling me that I meant something. He also helped me with small tasks, not doing them for me, but giving me tools to accomplish them myself.

The teacher I had for the last half of first grade accepted me and made me feel pride in myself for the first time and I think about that a lot.

An English professor in college actually critiqued my writing and taught me a lot about the craft. Most of my teachers before then just figured I was a good writer who they didn't have to teach at all.

One teacher who stands out is Mr. K., my sixth grade English teacher. He is the first one who taught us how to actually write. Whatever you do, you have to make sure you know your topic, voice and audience. Everything else is just busy work.

Yes, I have had several wonderful teachers. The commonality is that they care – they care about their work, they care about teaching, they care about you learning, and they care about you succeeding no matter how much effort it takes on their part.

Ms. P., my drama teacher in college, and Ms. E. , my voice teacher in college. Ms. E. helped me become more self-aware and both of them did not mind that I am quirky.

[My] second grade Special Ed teacher Miss B. She tried the hardest and gave me hope.

Yes, I had a math teacher who took the time to learn with me. We had no idea about the NLD at this point, but she took the time to make sure I understood everything.

My 9th grade history teacher was just out of college and I felt that I had a connection to her. She was a mentor all throughout my high school years and helped me with everything.

Yes, the teachers who changed my life were the ones who "got" me when no one else did.

One math teacher knew I just couldn't do math and he let me pass if I wrote him a poem about math instead of doing the problems. It probably wasn't ethical but I was a good student otherwise and he knew that failing me would ruin my chances for college.

Mrs. Rose, my eighth grade music teacher, saw my creative side and encouraged me to continue playing the piano, even though I flunked band (trying to play the tuba). Now, how many people do you know who actually flunked band? It is due to her that I am still a musician today. Otherwise, I would have been too discouraged to continue.

Yes. Teachers who genuinely cared and showed that they did. Teachers who hugged me during a meltdown. Teachers who praised me – I lived for praise. Teachers who let me use their room to eat lunch in or cool down when I needed a break.

In this chapter, we have looked at many of the ways both parents and teachers can help us. But much of our success depends upon ourselves. In Chapter Six, we answer some of your questions, and share with you some strategies and tips that worked for us.

Chapter Six:
(Some of) Your Questions Answered

Being able to tell your parents and teachers what you need and how they can help you is the first step in learning to advocate for yourself. And that is a good start toward living the independent life you hope to lead someday. In the meantime, the next step is to learn some concrete, specific skills to help you with some of the more challenging aspects of having NLD.

One of the most frustrating things about growing up with NLD is that you don't know what you don't know. That is, most neurotypical teens seem to at least grasp the scope of what they still have to learn, but those of us with NLD may not. So here are some questions that have puzzled many of us. In this Second Edition, I also have included the most frequently-asked questions sent in by readers of the First Edition, and have organized all of these by topic.

Physical and Mental Health

Q. I feel like everybody and everything is always stressing me out. Is there anything I can do?

We learned in Chapter Four how the stress around us can take its toll on our self-esteem and lead to learned helplessness. In Chapter Five, we learned how to make our family, friends, teachers, and doctors aware that it was taking a toll on us so that they could know how to stop exacerbating the problem. Now we get to the heart of the problem, which, for better or for worse, means more talk about the brain. So here's how stress works. As soon as the amygdala senses danger, from whatever source, it conveys to the hypothalamus a basic message: "Danger, danger, do something!"

At that point, the hypothalamus sends a signal to the adrenal glands, located at the top of the kidneys, to release glucocorticoids, or stress hormones. The first stress hormone released is adrenaline (also called epinephrine), which makes your heart beat faster, your blood pressure rise, your body sweat, etc. The second, perhaps more dangerous stress hormone, is cortisol.[57]

And while acute stress may act as a temporary pain relief, chronic stress does the reverse, as a constant bombardment of glucocorticoids frequently can lead to high blood pressure, heart attack, stroke, and weakened immune system function.[58] Also, chronic stress can even destroy the BDNF that makes your brain work, and when the BDNF is attacked, so is the ability to learn effectively.[59]

So what is the solution? One is simple: exercise. Countless studies show that exercise improves your heart, lowers your blood pressure, and strengthens your immune system. Exercise actually can improve your brain function, reduce anger,[60] help you to learn better, and even improve your grades![61]

Microbiologist John Medina explains how exercise helps you get rid of stress:

> When you exercise, you increase blood flow across the tissues of your body. This is because exercise stimulates the blood vessels to create a powerful, flow-regulating molecule called nitric oxide. As the flow improves, the body makes new blood vessels [...]. This allows more access to the bloodstream's goods and services, which include food distribution and waste disposal. The more you exercise, the more tissues you can feed and the more toxic waste you can remove. This happens all over the body. That's why exercise improves the performance of most human functions [...] The same happens in the human brain.[62]

As for how much exercise, the general rule of thumb is that we need at least 30 minutes of vigorous exercise per day. What type of exercise you do, that is entirely up to you, but if you need some suggestions, here are a few:

- Walking: Whether taking a stroll around the neighborhood, doing laps around a track with your iPod cranked up, or walking your dog, this is one of the most therapeutic, gentle-to-your-body, tried-and-true forms of exercise. The speed, direction, and company – whether human or animal – are all up to you.

- Dancing: You can take classes in trendy new dances like NIA or Zumba, or go old-school and just blast your favorite CD and dance free-style at home. There's something for everyone. However, use caution about going into nightclubs, especially if you have sensory sensitivity issues pertaining to light or sound.

- Biking: Riding your bike on the road or on a trail, or even riding a stationary bike is a good way to use all your major muscle groups.

- Swimming: Doing laps, diving, playing water games, or working out in the water can be a really fun way to exercise.

Obviously, there are many different forms of exercise from which to choose, including both team sports and individual pursuits. But whatever the activity and intensity level, from shooting hoops to shooting pool to skeet shooting, the goal is to find an enjoyable way to move around.

Q. How can I remind myself to eat healthfully and exercise every day?

One way is to find a plan that works for you and put everything onto one page that you can print and check off each day. Here is a sample chart for a mostly vegetarian diet that you can easily adapt to your needs. Each little check box represents one serving of the designated food group. There also are spaces to record your daily exercise and water intake.

Daily Food Intake and Exercise Chart

Date: Exercise: Stretch: Strength:

Dairy: 90 to 120 cal (low fat add 1 E, whole fat add 2 E)	[ ]	[ ]	[ ]			
Protein: 45 to 80 cal	[ ]	[ ]	[ ]	[ ]	[ ]	[ ]
Grain: 60 to 100 cal	[ ]	[ ]	[ ]	[ ]	[ ]	
Vegetable: 10 to 40 cal	[ ]	[ ]	[ ]	[ ]	[ ]	
Fruit: 80 to 100 cal	[ ]	[ ]				
Extras: 30 to 70 cal	[ ]	[ ]	[ ]	[ ]	[ ]	[ ]	[ ]
Water	[ ]	[ ]	[ ]	[ ]	[ ]	[ ]

Dairy: 1 C. non-fat yogurt - ½ C. low-fat cottage cheese (plus 1 E) - 1 C non-fat milk - 1 oz hard cheese (plus 1 E) – ½ C ice cream (plus 2 E) – ½ cup low- or non-fat frozen yogurt (plus 1 E)

Protein: 2 oz cod – 1 oz salmon – ½ C cooked beans – 2 T hummus – 1 egg (plus 1 E) – 2oz tofu – 1 oz or 3 Tablespoons nuts (plus 1 E) – 1 Tablespoon peanut butter (plus 2 E) - 2 strips - 2 links - 1 hot dog - 2oz tuna – 1 veg. sausage patty

Grain: 1 slice (1 oz) bread – ½ pita – ½ small bagel (1 oz) – ¼ large bagel – ½ English muffin, hamburger bun – ½ C cooked rice, pasta or cereal – 5 Triscuits – 6" tortilla or .75 8" tortilla – 1 oz pretzels – 3 C air-popped corn -1 C unsweetened cereal – 1/3 C croutons – 4 whole grain crackers – ¼ C granola (+ 1 E.)

Vegetable: ½ cup cooked green, carrots, squash, eggplant, mushrooms, red cabbage, cauliflower – 2 cups lettuce, raw cabbage, raw spinach – 1 cup sprouts – 4 Brussels sprouts – ½ med artichoke – ½ c raw chopped veg – 6 spears asparagus – 1 medium or 6 baby carrots – 4 celery stalks – ½ ear corn – ¼ cup corn, peas, mashed potato (plus E if butter) – 1 tomato or onion or ½ c chopped – ½ small baked potato or sweet – 6 oz vegetable juice – 1 C veg soup – ½ C tomato sauce (+ 1 E if oil) – 3 T salsa

Fruit: 1 medium apple, orange, peach – 1 small banana – 6 oz juice – ½ cup canned or cut-up – ½ grapefruit – 2 Tablespoons raisins – ½ mango – 1 cup melon, whole berries, cherries, grapes (1/2 c if sliced) – ¼ cup dried fruit

Extras: ¼ C. sorbet - 6 oz soda - 1 teaspoon oil, butter, marg - 1 Tablespoon cream cheese or sour cream – 2 T. low-fat sour cream – 2 teaspoons sugar, jam, honey, chocolate syrup – ½ oz chocolate – 3 hard candies – 1 cookie, 1-2" diam. - 3 graham crackers – 5 chips – 1 Tablespoon salad dressing

Combos: cheese pizza (1/8 of 12" pie) = 1 G, 1 ½ D, 2 E – mac & cheese (1 Cup) = 2 G, 1 ½ D, 3 E – fruit pie (1/8 of 9" pie) = 1 F, 1 G, 3 E – Chocolate cake (1/12 of 9" cake with frosting) = 1 G, 4 E.

Q. How can I find a therapist who is right for me and who understands people with NLD?

Like other kinds of referrals, the most effective way to find a good therapist is to ask other people with NLD who have had a good experience in therapy and who are satisfied with their therapist. If you don't know anyone to ask, you can try getting a referral from your family doctor, if he or she is sufficiently familiar with you and the issues raised by having NLD. For most of us who have health insurance, the choice of therapist will be informed by which therapists are included in the insurance company's network (otherwise, the insurance company will not pay for therapy).

Most insurance companies will provide a list of therapists, sorted by location and specialty. Usually, if you see among the specialties "ADHD," "learning disabilities," or "autism," these therapists may be more likely to have an understanding of NLD. But the best bet is to call and ask. Even then, as you have read in Chapter Five, there are many therapists who just do not work for us and/or do not understand NLD at all.

Before you commit to therapy, I highly recommend that you pick up a copy of Asperger Syndrome and Anxiety by Dr. Nick Dubin,[63] so you know how to talk about your issues in an effective way. Chapter Seven of his book answers the question at hand, of how to find a therapist that is right for you. But you first should read Chapters Three and Four so you know what kind of therapy may be appropriate. The rest of his book gives good explanations of how various situations may provoke or alleviate anxiety in people with Asperger's, including providing insight into how meltdowns are not entirely bad, but may actually be helpful. Overall, this book is an excellent resource for NLDers struggling with fear and anxiety.

Personal and Social Skills

Q. My parents insist that I improve my table manners. Why?

Q. Where can I find a guide to etiquette that actually takes into account the customs of the 21st century? And just what is etiquette anyway?

To answer the first question, it's hard to know what you look like eating unless you do it in front of a mirror. And when you gobble food, eat with your fingers, and eat the way you might do when you were alone, it looks kind of gross to others. Plus, your parents worry that if you have to eat in public, like at a restaurant or job interview, you won't know how to do it politely. You can learn the rules of etiquette, which are important to a lot of people, including the people who might hire you, admit you into their college, or who pay your bills. Then you have the option to "be correct" when you want to.

When you say the word "etiquette," many people think of Emily Post. Though she is long gone, her great granddaughter-in-law Peggy Post has continued her work and produced a number of very good, informative books on the subject. One of these, co-written with Emily Post's great granddaughter Cindy Post Senning and Sharon Watts, is <u>Teen Manners: From Malls to Meals to Messaging and Beyond</u>.[64] It covers these questions and just about everything else you need to know about manners, and more importantly for NLDers: why you need to know this stuff. The Emily Post Institute also has a website called "Teen Manners"[65] which gives excerpts from the book.

Another website called "RudeBusters!" billing itself as "A safe haven from rudeness, rage and stress"[66] has much useful information presented in an easy-to-understand manner.

Q. How do I actually find out how to read and interpret social cues?

Well, most of us are not too good at it. One good book, addressed to teens through adults is, <u>Will I Ever Fit In?: The Breakthrough Program for Conquering Adult Dyssemia</u> by Stephen Nowicki and Marshall P. Duke.[67] This book is very useful, in that it not only explains, but shows you how to improve in all aspects of nonverbal communication: gaze and eye contact, body space and touch, paralanguage (tone, loudness, and pace of speech), facial expression, gestures and postures, fashion and hygiene, social rules and norms, nonverbal receptivity, conversational skills, and timing and rhythm.

Q. How do I "dress for success," or for a date, for that matter?

Let's start with the basics. Everybody should practice good hygiene, including taking a shower or bath every day, keeping one's hair cut regularly and a neat hairstyle, shaving daily (guys), clean and trimmed nails, clean and pressed (or at least not wrinkled and torn) clothing. If you wear leather shoes, they should be polished; if not, shoes should at least be clean. Because some NLDers have sensory sensitivity issues, we like to wear our old, comfy clothes – sometimes even if they have holes in them! That's fine for hanging around the house or with your friends, if they also dress casually. But for "public appearances," like school, religious services, doctor visits, airplane travel, and going out with your parents, you should try to look appropriate.

As far as style, guys can check out Esquire Magazine's <u>The Handbook of Style: A Man's Guide to Looking Good</u>.[68] It covers just about all rules imaginable about clothes, from jeans to suits, haircuts to shoes, and everything in between. And it gives a really clear reason for every fashion rule, important for NLDers. Plus it's really funny. Strangely, I haven't found any similar books for women, so if you know of any, please let me know.

Q. Where and how can I even get a date? Is dating even possible for NLDers?

The whole dating scene can be very scary and frustrating for NLDers. Having trouble reading social cues can backfire in any number of ways. We may miss both jokes and actual overtures from possible dating partners, and far beyond the average biological period of latency, we may not even understand why others think sexual activity is pleasurable. And even if we are successful at getting a date, we may get dumped on early because we either come on too strong or because we act "clingy."

> *I only dated once in high school, and that was for the prom. After trying to find someone – anyone – who would go with me, I finally went with one of the relatively geeky girls … from the class above me … I thought she was a love interest. I tried to give her a present on Valentine's Day. I gave her this whole basket of Lindt chocolate truffles … And instead of returning any kind of favor, I mean, I didn't really expect to get kissed, but I thought she might at least give me a card or something. Instead, she just answered me by giving me one of those hugs that says, "Oh, don't worry, you'll get it right someday." Yeah, right… kind of one of those brush-offs … it was not even a "let's-be-friends" hug. It was more, "you are a totally freakin' idiot when it comes to this love thing, so … ok, I wish you well, but in the meantime, 'wouldn't you know it, I've got to go to second period'."*

Still, this does not necessarily mean that dating is out of the question. There are a few key approaches you might want to consider. The most obvious is to ask your friends and family to introduce you to someone who might be compatible with you. Or, you could try the "conventional" approach, which may not be the best approach. Perhaps you may have heard from your friends, parents, or even on TV that you should just walk up to a potential date, say something nice, and if she/he responds positively, you can take it from there. Well, this approach may work, but you have to know what to say, and many of us feel awkward or shy when it comes to making conversation. You might want to talk to a trusted neurotypical friend or sibling ahead of time, preferably of the same gender and sexual orientation as your potential date, and ask their advice on which conversation starters do and don't work well. You especially will want to think ahead of time about how much about yourself (including the fact that you have NLD) you want to disclose. If the person you are trying to meet does not know that you have NLD or does not understand it, this is a risky option, as they may leave or get angry for what seems no reason at all, but which may be "obvious" to him or her, even if it's something as simple as your not making eye contact.

The third approach is to try to convert an existing close friendship into a romantic partnership. The advantage here is that the potential love interest already knows you well enough to understand your NLD, and therefore knows not to not read too much into your occasional awkwardness or social gaffe. You will already have established mutual understanding and respect, as well as ways to spend time together – or you wouldn't be friends. The downside is that if the friendship blooms into romance and the romance eventually tanks, you've lost a friend as well as a partner.

And if none of those approaches work, you can use an online dating service. Online dating comes in all shapes and sizes. There are the standard "open to everyone" sites (you know, the ones you hear the commercials for), as well as those geared to special interests, race, or religion. There are several sites for those with disabilities, which means both physical and mental disabilities. There is even a website which reviews these disability dating sites.[69] It does not however, include any sites specifically geared to those with NLD, nor even learning disabilities in general. In his book <u>Asperger Syndrome and Anxiety</u>, Nick Dubin[70] lists three LD-related dating sites: <u>www.wrongplanet.net</u> (a message board-format site for all LDs but geared to those with Autism Spectrum Disorders), <u>www.aspiesforfreedom.net</u> (for those with AS), and <u>www.aspieaffection.com</u> (a dating site for those with AS). So while there is no NLD-specific site, these last three come close and are NLD-friendly.

So to answer the original question, yes, dating is indeed possible for NLDers. In the meantime, though, it is important to know that you don't have to have a boyfriend or girlfriend to be happy. Many of us have found that by engaging in activities we like, we are likely to meet someone with similar interests who also may be interested in us.

Q. Speaking of dating, where can I can some info about relationships? And what about the changes of puberty, sex, and sexuality?

The most straightforward and easiest to understand of all the books on the market are <u>The "What's Happening to My Body" Book for Boys</u>[71] and <u>The "What's Happening to</u>

My Body" Book for Girls[72] by Lynda Madaras and Area Madaras. Though aimed at younger readers (and you already may be past some of the physical changes the authors describe), these are useful, and answer some of your potentially embarrassing questions in a non-embarrassing way. For older teens and young adults, a good book is Changing Bodies, Changing Lives,[73] by Ruth Bell Alexander, and other co-authors of Our Bodies, Ourselves[74] (which I also recommend for older girls and women). Changing Bodies covers literally everything you might need to know about sexual development, sexual identity, and sexuality, from how to kiss to the complications of pregnancy. It also addresses other concerns a teen might have, such as eating disorders, how to handle peer pressure, gangs, and drugs and alcohol.

Q. That may be all well and good for Neurotypicals, but are any of these books that you recommend really going to be helpful for someone with NLD?

I'm not going to claim that I can sum up all the answers in one chapter – far from it! Obviously, there are many lingering questions that you, the reader, still have, so many that it would take another whole book to answer them all. Fortunately, I can tell you the name of that book: Growing Up on the Spectrum: A Guide to Life, Love, and Learning for Teens and Young Adults with Autism and Asperger's by Lynn Koegel, Ph.D. and Claire LaZebnik.[75] This excellent book covers all sorts of things that you need to know, like conversation skills, self-management, bullying, dating, how to throw a party, and much more.

Organization Skills

Q. What are some helpful study techniques when you have NLD?

There seem to be three ways people with NLD can study effectively. The first is **auditory memorization**, or learning from listening or from reading aloud:

I read the material out loud into a tape recorder and then listen to it in order to review for tests, etc.

I read my notes into a tape recorder and then listened to them over and over again. If any teachers gave us essay questions in advance, I made sure to answer them and then memorize my answer.

The second technique is **visual memorization**, or reading what you are studying:

Read over my notes, read the relevant material, looking for alternative explanations of the material online. I prefer to read whenever possible, as I hate making "flash cards."

Reviewing the notes for all tests except math. In math I did lots of practice problems.

Simply reading over the material. As my organizational skills are poor, I never developed any complex study skills. The more I am interested in the material, the more I will soak it up. If I am not interested or if there is a heavy emphasis on visual material, the motivation is simply not there but I do what I have to do to pass.

I have a system, but I can't describe it, it's too hard. It was taught to me. It involves writing down each category, Introduction, Part I, then in each category breaking it down further, i.e., a, b, c, d, and into i, ii, iii, iv, etc.

Using flashcards, using color-coded pens to write (e.g. using a different color for headings, different color for vocabulary words).

Flashcards were extremely useful for studying vocab, both for foreign language classes and for the SATs. Also in terms of reviewing for a final, using the Outline mode in Microsoft Word. That way, you can organize your notes into categories, subcategories, etc. Reading straight through the textbook has only worked for me in history classes.

We also used **group study and/or a combination of the other** techniques:

Groups, where studying was done casually.

Being quizzed through auditory memory by someone else, memorization, discussion with classmates.

Making an outline of what to study – being able to talk over the subject aloud with someone – reading the textbooks/notes aloud – having someone quiz me verbally, and prompting me for things I forget – making mnemonics and songs about information.

Reading aloud, writing summaries and telling others what I learned (even my imaginary friends).

Writing notes, and then returning to my room to type on the computer, reviewing three times, and studying with partners sometimes.

Q. I can't write fast enough to take notes. What should I do?
Q. I write down everything, but don't know how to use the notes I take.

Both of these situations are a challenge. We may write so slowly that note-taking is physically difficult or impossible, or we may have trouble both writing and listening at the same time:

I don't take notes, both because I write incredibly slowly, and also because if I focus too much on writing, I can't focus on what is being taught. So I only write something down if it's a definition or something I can't get elsewhere, something visual like a flow chart.

Or, we may write fast enough, but have difficulty being able to pick out the salient points:

I try, but almost never take notes worth looking at again.

Yes. I write fast, and just write everything down that I can. (A friend used to say, "When the teacher tells us to take out our notebooks, you take yours out and write 'take out your notebooks'!" ;-)

I wrote EVERYTHING down and I kept the notes per subject in one single folder.

Yes, I did take notes, but I never learned a good system or went back to study them much.

I do take notes, although I tend to write down much more than I needed. Never have gotten a great system – I never know what information is important and what is not. Oh well, grad school is over in 2 months anyway.

This respondent summed up both challenges very well:

No, never. I could not write fast enough, and even if I could, I could not write and pay attention at the same time. I could never figure out which things the teacher was saying were most important.

So what do we do? Some of us **use technology** to help us:

I have an alpha smart. In high school when I had access to a laptop but didn't want to bring it to class, I seldom wrote any notes. I have developed the ability to be a quick and efficient typist and I can take very thorough notes with my alpha smart. I find carrying a laptop around and having to plug it in to be too much of a hassle and that is why an alpha smart is ideal.

Keeping all notes electronically is downright mandatory, as I'm unable to organize papers easily. With all of my notes stored on Google Docs, I simply search for the topic I need, and the information is readily available from anywhere.

Or we call on **our friends** or **an aide**:

No. I can't keep up if I do. I mooch off my friends' notes, they're usually pretty cool about running off photocopies.

I tried, but I could not write fast enough. Instead I would underline or highlight parts of the texts, or borrow notes from a friend.

In high school, I found it very hard to write while the teacher was talking. The teacher always spoke fast, and by the time I interpreted it and wrote it down, the teacher was already way ahead. In college, I qualify for note takers. This facilitates things since I can read the text to prepare and then just listen in class.

We may draw upon a combination of **other people and technology**:

Memorizing every word that is spoken and asking people what this means then memorizing that with the original speech. Could never write well enough to take notes, tape recorder worked well but the background noise made it impossible to listen to. Laptop computer would have worked and is my new plan.

Some of us ask our **teachers** to structure lectures to match our needs:

Yes, and the system that works best is if the teacher had notes available to look at while lecturing and to take home for me to type up on the computer.

So while note-taking may always continue to be a challenge for those of us with NLD, you can try using technology, asking your teacher to provide a lesson outline, asking friends for help, or requesting an aide.

Q. Papers – ugh! Is there anything that can help me with longer assignments?

One respondent describes the difference **good teaching** can make:

All the way through high school, when I was given an assignment, I would just sit and stare at the blank page, hoping and waiting for inspiration to strike. If it didn't, I just would be paralyzed. I knew I couldn't write a paper. It never occurred to me that other people had trouble too, that they did bad first drafts. I thought everyone else just had great ideas, and they could write starting from Point A to Point Z, writing a perfect paper on the first try. No one thought to tell me that this was not true. If I couldn't write perfectly on the first try, I would just shut down and not do the assignment at all. I got a lot of "zeros" and flunked every single English course in high school for that reason. I finally learned in college Freshman English how to write a paper. Pick a topic, express it in one or two sentences. Then write down about 4-6 thoughts that support that topic. Then make an outline, then write. My Freshman English teacher required us to turn in every step along the way so we couldn't skip any. Topic sentence – turn it in. Supporting ideas – turn them in. Paragraphs, first draft, revisions – she looked at every step. I started getting As on every paper using this method. Learning this technique completely improved my academic performance in all subjects, not to mention my self-esteem.

In addition to being lucky enough to have effective teachers, we have figured out methods that work for us.

My writing skills are very poor. My spoken voice is much better, therefore I plan to use voice transcribing software when I continue my education.

Some of us use a "**scatter shot**" method that involves writing down one idea, then another idea, and so on, and then trying to use a transition sentence to make all these disparate ideas flow into the main idea. This is probably the least effective method of getting a paper done. Because many people with NLD also tend to be perfectionists, it can take a *really* long time to get a paper done using this method.

When I have a paper assigned, I try to allow myself one full day to produce a page of writing.

I usually talk about it out loud (either to myself or someone else). I usually also need a day or two off. And a lot of times, I need to read a lot (of anything) first.

I start writing whatever comes to mind, then I revise multiple times by inserting the necessary information and correcting the grammar and structure.

Before I write a paper, I give myself a vague idea of what my arguments will be and then I start writing. I never have made outlines with any degree of detail. This system has allowed for me to get Bs for the most part. I think my difficulty with organizing and my tendency to stray from the initial essay question has prevented me from excelling beyond that.

Some of us use either low-tech methods or more advanced **technology** to help us with our writing:

I write all the facts on index cards, then I categorize the cards and make piles. From there, I start writing.

I begin by making a short informal list of topics I need to cover, and the order I should cover them in. Then, I use a distraction-free word processor called DarkRoom to freewrite my thoughts, going through multiple iterations of the same section or idea. After I develop a basic idea of how the essay should look, I paste the text into Microsoft Word and organize from there.

My computer is my best friend. I can't put it much better than that.

Or we may use a technique called **mind mapping**, a particular form of brainstorming. It is basically a kind of flow chart, in which you write down ideas on one topic, then on others, and then using lines and arrows, you make connections between and among ideas which have a causal link.

First, I brainstorm and write down every word that comes up. Then I write down the structure of the paper: section one = introduction, section two = etc. Then I start writing.

In college I knew it would take me a LOT longer to write papers so I allowed a lot of extra time. I finally figured out a system of making a graph or chart of what I was writing about, then what points supported the main point, then details and quotes from other sources.

Dumping and then having someone edit to make sure that it sounds correct, spider diagrams helped to get ideas out and organized by topic. Started in the middle and then went back to the beginning to write a thesis statement.

One good book that talks about mind mapping is <u>Learning Outside The Lines: Two Ivy League Students With Learning Disabilities And ADHD Give You The Tools</u>.[76] Written by Jonathan Mooney and David Cole, who, as the title suggests, speak from experience about what it is like to attend college when you have an LD, it gives lots of practical tips about study skills, note-taking and life away from home. And the book is extremely well-organized, making easy to use.

Outlining consists of making a list of topics you want to cover, then listing subtopics under each general topic, then writing proofs for each subtopic.

I pour all my thoughts out, and then systematically organize my papers. I have done very well in English, excelling in essays.

Introduction – point 1 – subpoints – point 2 – subpoints – point 3, 4, conclusion.

First, come up with a thesis. Then come up with three to five points to support the thesis. Then three to five sub-points for each of those. And then for each of the sub-points, make sure you have supporting quotes or data. Then the rest is just adding transition sentences to connect the main thoughts to one another. Then, write the conclusion and then write the abstract if one is needed. Then I make sure that I have it edited for me, first for content, then I write the next draft, then have it edited and proofread.

Q. Are there any examples of worksheets or lists that can help me write a paper?

Sure! Here are a few we have found to be helpful. Also, if our parents are willing to provide the rewards, some also find it useful and fun to build in a reward system for each step, or for finishing a project. If not, we can create our own rewards, such as taking a break, buying a pizza, going for a walk, watching a movie, or listening to favorite music.

Worksheet 1: Steps to Organizing a Research or Essay Paper

1. **Get assignment** (from class syllabus or when it's given).
2. Immediately **read the entire assignment** for clarity. If you have any questions, ask the teacher/professor.
3. Figure out the exact **steps you will need** to take in order to complete the assignment correctly and on time, using this model as a template.
4. **Calculate** approximately how long each of the steps will take.
5. **Schedule** each step and the time allowed into your master calendar. Allow **five hours** of writing time to produce a good draft of one page, exclusive of research and planning time.)
   Repeat Steps 1 through 5 for each assignment you now have in hand, even ones that are due after this assignment. The reason for this is that you probably will be doing early steps of later assignments at the same time you are completing an earlier assignment. Now, back to the first paper due. **Choose a topic** (if it is an essay), or **find and read** the book or books (if it is an analysis). Is it a novel or popular book that you can get **on CD**?
6. Find and read the **primary sources** (if it is a research paper).
7. If necessary, get topic **approved** by teacher/professor.
8. Look at the assignment again. If there is a choice of questions, **choose one question**.
9. **Create your thesis** and write it in one sentence.
10. Write **3-5 sentences** (depending on length of final paper) that support your thesis.
11. From library or Internet, **find secondary sources**. How many will you need? Which are most appropriate?
12. Look through or **read secondary sources**, marking good quotes with highlighter or Post-it notes.
13. Begin to **write the draft**. From this point on, plan on needing **five hours** to produce **one page** of writing.
14. **Re-read the assignment**. Be sure you are answering the question completely and thoroughly.
15. When draft is finished, you can **send it out to aide or tutor** for edit/proof.
16. **Make edits** and any changes.
17. Create **bibliography** or works cited page.
18. Create any **handouts**, visuals, illustrations, charts, notes for oral presentation, etc. that may be required.
19. Produce **final draft** and turn in early or on time.
20. **Pat yourself** on the back. Get a reward or treat!
21. Get busy on the **next paper** or project.

Worksheet 2: Organizing an Essay or Research Paper (with rewards and checklist)

1. Get assignment (from class syllabus or when given). Read all the syllabi on the first day of each class and put a check mark next to each writing assignment.

How long will this take?_____ Due date for this step?_____

When will I do this step?_____ Reward points_____

    Completed ☐

2. Immediately **read the entire assignment** for clarity. If questions, ask professor.

How long will this take?_____ Due date for this step?_____

When will I do this step?_____ Reward points_____

    Completed ☐

3. Figure out the exact **steps you will need** to take in order to complete the assignment correctly and on time, using this model as a template.

How long will this take?_____ Due date for this step?_____

When will I do this step?_____ Reward points_____

    Completed ☐

4. Calculate approximately how long each of the steps will take.

How long will this take?_____ Due date for this step?_____

When will I do this step?_____ Reward points_____

    Completed ☐

5. Schedule each step and write down the time allowed into your master calendar. Allow **five hours** of writing time to produce a good draft of one page, exclusive of research and planning time.

How long will this take?_____ Due date for this step?_____

When will I do this step?_____ Reward points_____

    Completed ☐

Repeat Steps One through Five for each assignment you now have in hand, even ones that are due after this assignment. The reason is that you probably will be doing early steps of later assignments at the same time you are completing an earlier assignment.

6. Now, back to the first paper due.

    a) **Choose a topic** (if essay),

How long will this take?_____ Due date for this step?_____

When will I do this step?_____ Reward points_____

    Completed ☐

    b) and/ or **find**

How long will this take?_____ Due date for this step?_____

When will I do this step?_____ Reward points_____

    Completed ☐

    c) and **read** the book or books (if analysis). Is it a novel or popular book that you can get **on tape**? If so, ask the library to get it for you.

How long will this take?_____ Due date for this step?_____

When will I do this step?_____ Reward points_____

    Completed ☐

7. Find and read the **primary sources** (if research).

How long will this take?_____ Due date for this step?_____

When will I do this step?_____ Reward points_____

    Completed ☐

8. If necessary, get your topic **approved** by teacher or professor.

How long will this take?_____ Due date for this step?_____

When will I do this step?_____ Reward points_____

    Completed ☐

9. Look at the assignment again. If there is a choice of questions, **choose one question**.

How long will this take?_____ Due date for this step?_____

When will I do this step?_____ Reward points_____

    Completed ☐

10. **Create your thesis** and write it in one sentence.

How long will this take?_____ Due date for this step?_____

When will I do this step?_____ Reward points_____

    Completed ☐

11. Write **3-5 sentences** (depending on length of final paper) that support your thesis.

How long will this take?_____ Due date for this step?_____

When will I do this step?_____ Reward points_____

    Completed ☐

12. From library or Internet, **find secondary sources**. How many will you need? Which are most appropriate?

How long will this take?_____ Due date for this step?_____

When will I do this step?_____ Reward points_____

    Completed ☐

13. Look through or **read secondary sources**, marking good quotes with highlighter or Post-it notes.

How long will this take?_____ Due date for this step?_____

When will I do this step?_____ Reward points_____

    Completed ☐

14. Begin to **write the draft**. From this point on, plan on needing **five hours** to produce **one page** of writing.

How long will this take?_____ Due date for this step?_____

When will I do this step?_____ Reward points_____

Completed ☐

15. **Re-read the assignment**. THIS IS CRITICAL! Be sure you are answering the question completely and thoroughly.

How long will this take?_____ Due date for this step?_____

When will I do this step?_____ Reward points_____

Completed ☐

16. When the draft is finished, you can **send it to your aide or tutor** for edit/proof.

How long will this take?_____ Due date for this step?_____

When will I do this step?_____ Reward points_____

Completed ☐

17. **Make edits** and changes.

How long will this take?_____ Due date for this step?_____

When will I do this step?_____ Reward points_____

Completed ☐

18. Create **bibliography** or works cited page.

How long will this take?_____ Due date for this step?_____

When will I do this step?_____ Reward points_____

Completed ☐

19. Create any **handouts,** visuals, illustrations, charts, notes for oral presentation, etc. that may be required.

How long will this take?_____ Due date for this step?_____

When will I do this step?_____ Reward points_____

    Completed ☐

20. Produce **final draft** and turn in early or on time.

How long will this take?_____ Due date for this step?_____

When will I do this step?_____ Reward points_____

    Completed ☐

21. Pat yourself on the back. **Get a reward** or treat!

How long will this take?_____ Due date for this step?_____

When will I do this step?_____ Reward points_____

    Completed ☐

22. Get busy on the **next paper** or project.

Worksheet 3: Super Reward Chart for Book Reports

(Note: *Hamlet* is used here as an example of an assigned reading. Adapt this sample chart by filling in your own assignments and your own rewards!)

Rewards for Completing Steps in Writing Analysis of *Hamlet*

This Task	If Completed by This Time	# Prize Points
1. Annotated Bibliography	**9:00 pm**, November 12	15 points
2. *Hamlet* – thesis + 3-5 supporting sentences + secondary source quotes marked with sticky notes + one page of first draft	**noon**, November 13	20 points
3. *Hamlet* pages 2-4 of first draft	**9:00 pm**, November 13	25 points
4. *Hamlet* page 5 of first draft	**10:00 am**, November 14	10 points
5. *Hamlet* page 6 of first draft	**4:00 pm**, November 14	10 points
6. *Hamlet* Completed first draft, submit to aide for edits	**3:00 pm**, November 16	40 points
7. *Hamlet*, works-cited page	**3:00 pm**, November 17	5 points

Rules: Task must be done in full, by time specified. **No partial points** *for partial task completion. All prize points must be redeemed by November 21.*

Rewards Redemption Chart

Lunch at restaurant of your choice	35 points
"Get out of weekly chores free" card	45 points
One Scrabble game	10 points
Trip to bowling alley	100 points
Movie of your choice in theater	50 points
Watch DVD of your choice	15 points
Order in take-out food	40 points
$20 credit at bookstore or music store	50 points

Q. Time management is really tough. I've even read books to try to improve, but they all seem to be written for people without NLD. Is there any help for me?

Well, yes and no. Most of us with NLD really resent having people tell us we need to "get organized." "Getting organized" seems like just one more frustration. But if you can get over the resentment, being organized – up to a point – really does save time and energy.

Because right now, going to school is your primary job, the skills discussed here have to do with organizing school-based projects. Some of the tips can be adapted to life at work, and all can be used for life at college.

Our respondents shared tips for using **planning tools**:

I write important dates and deadlines on a calendar that's clearly visible that I can't miss, so that way I don't usually!

I use my alarm a lot if I can't work on something longer than a certain time. When the alarm goes, I need to stop doing what I'm doing, no matter whether it is finished or not. Over time, I learned to check how much time I have left and I get sidetracked less. Still, I very often don't accomplish the goal in the time set.

This hasn't been a huge problem for me. I just make a list every day of what I have to accomplish, and also what is coming up in the future. The main problem is what things come up during the day that are NOT on the list. They tend to throw me off track.

I use Google Calendar to remember important dates and events, and I use RememberTheMilk to show tasks and due dates. Both show as modules on my Google homepage, so I'm constantly reminded of what I have to do. They're also both accessible from my phone, so I can add an event or task before I have the opportunity to forget it.

After YEARS of resistance, I finally got a calendar. I now write down all appointments, meetings, etc. when I make them, and then remember to look at the calendar every morning when I have my coffee. That way I don't forget places I have to go or people I have to call. I also write down long-term things, like "go see the dentist" six months ahead so I remember to make the appointment in a timely way. This has helped a lot. I wish I hadn't been such a stubborn fool for so long. It was because I am an artist and musician - and we creative types don't need to be bound by ordinary rules. Well, that would be fine if the rest of the world worked on artist-time, but after getting bounced from a couple of jobs and losing a couple of friends, I finally figured it out.

Some of us ask for **help or accommodations**:

I have a planner. I meet with an LD coach once a week.

Taking a lighter course load. Right now I am taking 60% of a full course load. This way, I am under MUCH less stress. Having to take at least one and likely two extra years [to finish college] is well worth being able to actually enjoy the courses that are of interest to me without being under the constant stress that even my non-NLD peers who take a full course load are under.

We **keep our lives simple**:

[Don't really have a system.] I make very few commitments, to avoid this one altogether.

Do the work. Forget there is such a thing called a social life.

And **sticking to a routine** really helps:

When I was in school it was best if I did my homework right after school. I also did harder assignments (like math) first, because I had more energy and also to get them out of the way.

Yes, once a routine is established, I do well.

Well, people ask how I can do grad school, my thesis, work four jobs and remember to live. I say it really helps to have no social life and no friends – which is true. You'd be amazed how much time people waste on friends (sarcastic). I make sure I get enough sleep, always, which helps, and I block out chunks for studying and chunks of break time, because if I don't take breaks when I should, I'll end up taking them when I have to or messing up at a job or something.

Yes. Every day I divide what needs to be done into the following categories: "Must do," "Should do," "Want to do," and "Coming Up." Then from the "Must do" list, I select one or two "Most important goals" for the day, and make sure I get to those first.

You also might try keeping a weekly chart of projects and write down when each is due. Here is an example:

TO DO Week of:

	When due?	Steps to complete?	Finish

HOMEWORK:

PAPERS/TESTS:

MEETINGS/APPOINTMENTS:

CALLS/LETTERS/EMAILS:

JOB/OTHER OBLIGATIONS:

Q. I have trouble keeping track of what I have to do every day. Is there some kind of a system I can use?

Try a simple daily "to-do" list. When you list on paper or on your computer all the things you have to do, they no longer clutter up your brain. The trick is to remember to make the list every night before bed, and then to look at it every morning. Pick no more than three Most Important Goals for the Day, then list the others in their order of importance. When you check off an item, you get a feeling of accomplishment! Here is an example:

TO DO: NOVEMBER 18

MOST IMPORTANT GOALS:

- o   Take a walk for 45 minutes
- o   Turn in Hamlet paper
- o   Call Grandma to wish her a happy birthday

MUST DO:

- o   Eat breakfast
- o   Take a shower and get dressed
- o   Go to school
- o   Answer emails
- o   Finish homework
- o   My turn to cook dinner tonight

SHOULD DO:

- o   Help fix Mom's computer
- o   Do a load of laundry
- o   Get hair cut this afternoon
- o   Start on the math assignment due next week.

WOULD LIKE TO DO:

- o   Take a nap
- o   Watch The Simpsons at 7:30

NEXT DAY/COMING UP:

- o   Start looking for a book for next book report

Q. I have so many projects and assignments in school this year, plus my normal chores at home. How can I remember everything I have to do?

Here is a system you may find helpful:

1. LIST

All the things you have to do or want to do, both current and near future, into one big list.

2. SORT by Priority

What has to be done right now or today? What has to be done tomorrow or the day after that? Are there deadlines attached to any of the other items? If so, what are they? Working backwards from each deadline, what are the steps necessary to make them happen on time?

OR

2. SORT by Project

For example: English paper on *Hamlet*, volunteer to help make Spanish club posters, making holiday cards for relatives and friends. Are there deadlines attached to any of these items? If so, what are they? Working backwards from each deadline, what are the steps necessary to make them happen on time?

3. DECIDE

Which items can be delegated or eliminated for now. Delegate or eliminate.

4. TRANSFER

Items onto your daily TO-DO list or onto your running TO-DO list. Add deadlines if applicable.

5. START DOING ITEMS.

When finished, check off. Transfer any undone daily TO-DO items to the next day's list. Keep working on your running list, moving things to daily list as needed per deadlines.

Alternatives to Public High School

Q. What if public school just isn't working for me? Are there any options for teens with NLD?

If you and your parents can stand to be together all day, every day, your family can consider home schooling. The late Sue Thompson wrote an excellent article about the pros and cons of home-schooling a student with NLD.[77]

If that is not an option, there are several private schools which are pretty good for those with LDs and even NLD. I am not really in the position to recommend schools, but the NLD discussion forums may offer you some help in finding a school that suits your needs.

Some school districts are now offering online instruction, so that you can complete your high school diploma without leaving home. While this may not be ideal in terms of building your social skills, it may be a feasible option for you. Contact your state's Department of Education for more information.

Thinking About Going On to College

Q. How do I survive the SAT?

Read <u>Up Your Score: The Underground Guide to the SAT, 2011-2012 Edition</u>.[78] Written and revised each year by four or five people who aced the SAT (the current version is written by Larry Berger, Michael Colton, Manek Mistry, Paul Rossi, and Jean Huang), this book gives a funny yet serious guide to the SAT, offers great mnemonics for the vocab words, tips on how and whether to cram, and tells a story about how this torture was thought up by the "Evil Testing Serpent" (ETS).

Also, that very same ETS (which really stands for "Educational Testing Service") has an excellent explanation on its web site[79] about what you need to know to document your disability in order to qualify for test accommodations. (Please note that you need to allow several months to get this documentation, send it in, and take the test, so you will want to find out about this process sometime in your sophomore year.)

Q. I know I want to apply to college. But the application process is overwhelming, and I am not sure what I'll find when I get there!

You have to be really organized to apply to college, and applying to more than one college is even more challenging. It helps to keep a chart or spreadsheet of all the colleges, their application deadlines (so you can give yourself plenty of time to meet them), the fees, and what else they require, such as essays and letters of reference.

We suggest starting this process no later than the summer before your senior year, so you don't have to be doing applications or writing application essays during the busy fall semester.

As far as what to expect at college, one resource is <u>College Success for Students with Learning Disabilities</u>.[80] In addition to giving good advice and lots of helpful hints, the book is really easy to read and to use.

One thing to keep in mind when choosing a college is that you might do well to find one that offers plenty of online classes. Online classes offer several advantages to those with NLD.

First, since you will be sitting at a computer and not in the classroom, your nonverbal language-reading disability will not get in the way of learning. Second, because online classes use a discussion forum format, you can reply as often as you want, making your posts as brief or as verbose as you choose, and no one will judge you for being a chatterbox – though if they do, they usually see it as "active participation." When you see the length of other students' posts, you can get a pretty good idea of how much is "too much." Third, you can replay the audio or video clips as often as you want, whereas in a regular classroom you might be judged negatively for having to have something explained to you again. And there is no need to take notes at all! Fourth, if you have light-sensitivity issues, and cannot use the computer for long periods of time, you can print out all the posts, look them over one at a time, and write out replies by hand, and then type or dictate them later on. Last, and perhaps most important, online classes have a flexible schedule. Obviously, there are deadlines for assignments and papers, but most are end-of-week, not end-of-day. So you can do the work when it suits you.

Q. I'm not so sure I am ready to live away from home. What to do?

It's tough to decide whether you are ready to live away from home. Many of us are not. An excellent resource is Leaving Home: Survival of the Hippest by Andie Parton and Lynn Johnston[81] (the latter is the artist of the comic strip "For Better or For Worse"). The book guides you through the ins and outs of living in a college dorm and in an apartment. It provides lots of great tips on subjects such as weeding out difficult roommates, dealing with landlords, making budgets, and more. Reading it will give you a good overview of the skills you need to live independently, and can help you decide if you feel ready.

Graduation day will be here before you know it. Many of your peers may be going off to summer jobs and then college. You know you are smart enough to go to college but both your parents – and even you yourself, if you're honest about it – may feel that you are not quite ready to leave home. I know it may be painful to hear, but remember that in terms of development, socially and emotionally you may be more like a neurotypical 14-year-old, even though your physical body is now 17 or 18. To give yourself time to catch up, you may need a little more time at home.

Some of the older respondents in this study went directly to college after high school, and fell flat on their faces – not because they couldn't keep up with the academic work, but because their self-discipline and organizational skills just weren't up to speed with their intellectual ability. Living in a dorm while attending college requires all of the above, plus the social savvy to deal with difficult roommates or people in the dorm who are driving you crazy.

I was doing OK in my classes, but the guy who lived in the next room played music all night so I couldn't get any sleep. Every night it was the same thing. Until midnight, he practiced his electric guitar. I tried banging on the walls, reporting him to the RA, but nothing worked. I was exhausted.

I hung out with a bunch of guys who I thought were pretty cool. Two of them seemed normal, but one of them was a stoner, even though it took a while for me to figure it out (I could tell from his glazed eyes and slurred speech). That was OK – I would just leave his room when he lit up. But one night, his mom came to visit. She brought in a pizza, and then opened a beer. I was pretty shocked when she lit up a joint, but then it got worse – she actually came on to me. I started to panic – I didn't know what to do. I tried to find a graceful way to leave, but I couldn't. So I just said "excuse me" and ran to my room. The worst part was the next day, when I found out that I could have been arrested simply for being in the presence of someone doing drugs, even though I didn't do them.

Some of us opted to attend a local 2-year or 4-year college within commuting distance of home. After the first couple of years, when we had enough experience to understand the demands of college work, we transferred to a different college, or moved onto the campus. How do you know you are ready for independent living? Here is a checklist. You and your parents may want to tailor it to your specific needs, adding any special issues you may have.

Self-Assessment: Are You Ready for Independent Living in the Dorm?

Academic:

- ❑ Are all current assignments completely up to date?

- ❑ Are you earning a "B" or better in all your classes?

- ❑ Are you keeping a calendar, with all long- and short-term assignments marked, so that you know the deadlines for papers, exams, and projects?

- ❑ On your calendar, are you designating appropriate amounts of time during the week in order to complete all assignments thoroughly and on time?

- ❑ Have you identified and engaged an appropriate source(s) of extra help (tutor, appointment with teaching assistants, conference with professor?)

- ❑ Have you availed yourself of the special accommodations offered in class (tutors, extra time for quizzes?)

Personal:

- ❑ Are you taking excellent care of your health, including taking any meds on time?

- ❑ Are you bathing or showering every day?

- ❑ Are you wearing clean underwear, socks, and clothes each day?

- ❑ Are you avoiding food and substances harmful to your health?

- ❑ Are you consistently making appropriate food choices, in order to maintain a normal weight?

- ❑ Have you found an *effective* method for getting eight hours of sleep every night?

- ❑ Do you wake up each morning on time, and get right to your daily routine (clean, dress, breakfast, work or class)?

- ❑ Do you have a regular exercise plan and implement it daily?

- ❑ Are your friends helpful, supportive and generally positive and healthy people?

- ❑ Do you have a regular method of stress reduction, such as meditation, prayer, or yoga?

- ❑ Do you have a method or support system or person to assist you with any emotional problem/crisis?

If, after reading this checklist, you honestly feel that you are not ready to leave home yet, you might very well consider at least starting your college degree by enrolling in one of the many online programs available. In addition to all the advantages described in the previous answer, online learning is extremely favorable for those who might have restrictive circumstances other than NLD, such as part-time work, a child or children, travel, a physical disability, or no means of transportation.

Q. Should I tell my teachers or professors about having NLD?

Whether you choose to tell your teachers is up to you. Some people think that their teacher might be prejudiced against them if they know they have a disability. But, it's better to be straightforward because that way, you can get the help you need, plus any accommodations for note-taking or testing, etc. If you are constantly raising your hand in class, but the teacher doesn't know you have NLD, he or she might think you are really interested in the class. On the other hand, the teacher might think that you are just a loudmouth. So it's better to tell. But since it's not that easy to talk about, it might be better to write a letter to your teacher telling him or her what you need. To help you get started, here is a sample letter, followed by a couple of samples of the kinds of accommodations you might need.

Dear Mr./Ms./Dr. _____,

I am a junior this year and I will be taking your class, (NAME OF CLASS).

I have Nonverbal Learning Disabilities, and would greatly appreciate you reading the following information about me, so that we can have a successful semester working together.

I also respectfully request the accommodations listed below. I appreciate your consideration, and welcome any questions you may have. My email is:_____

Thank you very much,

Your name

About my learning style and disabilities:

I am a very literal learner. Although I am able to understand abstractions in ideas, I am not that good at inferences. It is helpful to me if assignments and instructions for papers are given in writing and are specific and concrete. The fact that you are using BlackBoard is a big help to me.

Normally, I do not take many notes in class. This is not because I am not paying attention; I am. When I concentrate, I retain much of what I hear. If the material is also in the text book or the readings, so much the better. I write very slowly (and not too legibly), so quick note taking is too hard.

Although I am a lot better than I used to be at reading social cues, I sometimes still miss them. The main implication for your class is that I may not understand when to stop talking, especially if I am passionate about the topic at hand. It would be better for me if you are willing to say something like, "NAME, we are going to hear from someone else now," or telling someone else, "Let's hear what *you* have to say." If you use non-verbal cues (such as turning your body away from me or looking at another student) I may not be able to understand them. Please don't worry about hurting my feelings by telling me to shut up if necessary (some teachers have worried about this). I would rather you were blunt. This will prevent me from embarrassment and possible censure from fellow students.

Because I have difficulty with Executive Functioning and sequencing, longer written assignments such as those requiring research or multiple steps take me a very long time. I have found that I need to allow one full day to produce a page. Generally this is not a problem, as most teachers give such assignments well in advance. In order to produce essays in class, I need a lot of extra time both to organize my thoughts and because I write slowly. I normally take midterm and final exams at the Academic Advising Center.

SAMPLE ONE:

Accommodations I will need:
1. Midterm and final exam at the Academic Advising Center, as noted above.
2. Extra time to produce any written work (such as quizzes) given in class.
3. Take home assignments or tests given with sufficient lead time (at least one full day per page required.)

SAMPLE TWO:

Accommodations for learning:

a. **Untimed tests** in a distraction-free environment.

b. Limited computer time – to rest eyes **frequently** (accommodation necessary only if in-class computer use or tests given on the computer)

c. **Time management** tutor or "buddy" – for courses with written assignments that extend over time (e.g. papers) and for courses with multiple, simultaneous written assignments. Need help to look at all assignments, break them down into manageable parts, assign **interim due dates** to each, and report to tutor or "buddy" as each part is complete. I can do each part without help; it's the overall sequencing and time management that is difficult. For papers, need some help with **final editing** for continuity and flow. Help is not usually needed for short writing assignments such as those assigned at one class and due at the next, nor for math or science assignments.

d. **Audiobooks** for novels, short stories, longer readings in social sciences. Not needed for physical sciences or mathematics.

e. I tend to be **very literal**, and take people and things at face value. Sometimes but not always, this can cause a difficulty in communicating.

Q. This may sound silly, but is there anything to eat at college besides pizza, fries, and the salad bar (however great those might be)?

Yes! Most colleges have a wide selection of food and beverages at every meal, including options for special diets, such as vegetarian, vegan, kosher, and gluten-free. Plus, there are lots of ways to prepare tasty meals from what's available if you don't see something you like.

One of my favorite books is Tray Gourmet: Be Your Own Chef in the College Cafeteria by Larry Berger and Lynn Harris.[82] They and various contributing college students provide some rather spectacular and delicious recipes made from the standard cafeteria fare. Recipes range from the simple (making the hard-boiled eggs into deviled eggs, spicing up otherwise boring tuna fish sandwiches, etc.) to making really elaborate burgers, and fancy sundaes for dessert. Even if you don't make the recipes, you still will love many of the names (e.g. "Nietzsche's Nachos" or "Plato's Pita Pocket") and their complementary illustrations by Chris Kalb. The book also gives tips on stuff like dieting (and lack thereof), the pros and cons of caffeine, and how to grow your own culinary herbs.

Q. Before I choose potential colleges, how do I know which ones have the best Disability Services departments?

Although all colleges and universities are required by law to provide services, not all do so equally well. If you are applying to a college in the US, an excellent resource is Learning How to Learn: Getting Into and Surviving College When You Have a Learning Disability by Joyanne Cobb.[83] The back of the book lists all the colleges, ranked by effectiveness and price, that offer good LD services. The beginning of the book gives lots of information on the rights and accommodations to which you are entitled under the Americans with Disabilities Act (ADA) and Individuals with Disabilities Education Act (IDEA). The author also reminds you (or more to the point, reminds your parents) that where you get your degree (and what goes on your résumé) does not necessarily have to be the place where you *start* college. So don't stress about getting into the "best" name-brand or Ivy League school right now. You can always transfer later if you qualify and if that's what you want to do.

Earning a Living

Q. When I finish high school, how can I get health insurance?

Under the provisions of President Obama's Health Care Reform Bill of 2009, you can be covered on your parents' policy until you are age 26. However, most insurance companies also have a clause which will cover a "disabled dependent child" of any age. As long as you are single, not working, and living at home, you may be eligible to remain on your parents' policy. However, not all of us are comfortable with that nomenclature. We don't like to think of ourselves as "disabled" or "dependent," but if we are unable to work, and with the price of insurance going up rapidly, it is something to consider.

When you start work full-time, you will want to look for a company that offers good insurance and other benefits, in addition to a decent salary.

Q. How can I and my parents plan for my financial future?

Those with NLD who may be unable to work, or who may not be able to work full-time, are at a disadvantage when it comes to saving for our future. Unlike most young adults, if we don't work, we don't contribute into the Social Security system. We also cannot put money into Roth IRAs or other tax-advantaged savings accounts, which depend on earned income. We may get years behind in our retirement savings – not something most of us worry about when we are in high school. But it is important, because compound interest on our savings throughout the years is a key factor in having enough money to live on when we are old.

In terms of financial planning, your family might want to look into setting up a "Supplemental Needs Trust," which protects assets for your use in case you are now receiving or may ever need to receive government disability assistance. You will need to discuss this issue with an attorney, preferably one who specializes in the area of "Elder Law."[84]

Q. College is not for me. How can I find a good job that is "NLD friendly," and what do I tell my employer about having NLD?

Go get a copy of Yvona Fast's <u>Employment for Individuals With Nonverbal Learning Disabilities and Asperger's Syndrome</u>.[85] Written by an adult with NLD, this book is by far one of the best NLD-related books on the market. Not only does Fast list good and bad jobs for those with NLD and AS, with clear explanations of what makes them well-suited or poorly suited, but she also provides the reader with many first-hand testimonies from the NLDers and Aspies about why their current/previous jobs did or did not suit them.

Q. If I should encounter workplace discrimination because of my NLD, am I protected under the ADA?

Good question, especially considering that the status of NLD as a "real" LD is still in question. As of this writing, NLD is not yet in the DSM-IVTR (though, as previously mentioned, it probably will show up in the DSM-V in 2012). So here is what you need to know about the Americans with Disabilities Act:

The roots of the ADA lie in the Rehabilitation Act of 1973, a civil rights statute for government workers and contractors, and people who received government-granted financial aid, all of whom had disabilities (then called "handicaps").[86] It is from the Rehabilitation Act that we get the idea of "being on disability," meaning that one was receiving aid from the government, either permanently or until such time as the individual was able to work again.

Then came the 1989 proposal of the Americans with Disabilities Act, the premise of which was to protect people with disabilities from discrimination on account of their disabilities. It received strong bipartisan support in both the House and the Senate, and when President Bush signed it into law on July 26, 1990, he and the vast majority of Congress were pleased. Senator Orrin Hatch (R-Utah) called it "historic legislation." The late Senator Edward Kennedy (D-Massachusetts) even went so far as to call it an "emancipation proclamation" for people with disabilities.[87]

Yet in a 2000 survey, it was shown that 97% of disability-based employment discrimination lawsuits were ruled in favor of the employer.[88] So what went wrong?

When the ADA was drafted, it defined the term "disability" in the exact words the Rehabilitation Act used to define the term "handicap:" (1) a physical or mental impairment that substantially limits one or more of the major life activities of such an individual; (2) a record of such an impairment; or (3) being regarded as having such impairment.[89]

Not too much to worry about, right? But remember what I said in Chapter One, regarding what the "D" in "LD" stands for – that: "... labeling it a 'disability' makes it sound as though the child once had the ability but was rendered inoperative?" Well, that was the problem. The Federal Courts, most noticeably the Supreme Court, noticed the language of the Rehabilitation Act in the definition of disability in the APA, and assumed that if you were to prove in a Federal Court that you had a disability, it was "obvious" that you were trying to prove you were eligible to "be on disability" and hence, "collect disability payments."

As a result, the Courts determined that the phrase "substantially limits one or more of the major life activities" should be taken as literally and seriously as possible (since government payments were at stake), thereby making it nearly impossible for people to prove that they had a disability. But what got completely lost in the process was the fact that these were not meant to be subsidy cases; they were meant to be civil rights cases. The plaintiffs did not want to be out of work collecting government money; they wanted to be back at the jobs they had before they were fired unjustly. Clearly, this had to be corrected somehow.

Enter the 2008 Americans with Disabilities Act Amendments Act (ADAAA), which was passed a mere six weeks after the First Edition of this book was published. The first major change from the old ADA is that the ADAAA now covers those with disabilities that were once not "major enough" to "substantially limit" an individual's life or lifestyle. The new conditions covered include, but are not limited to: HIV, epilepsy, intellectual and developmental disabilities, Post Traumatic Stress Disorder, diabetes, multiple sclerosis,[90] heart attacks, bi-polar disorder, major depressive disorder, needing an oxygen tank, vertigo, back injury, and depression and anxiety.[91]

So, what does all this mean for someone with NLD? As to the original question of whether you are protected under the ADA, the answer is: you didn't used to be, but now you probably are. Probably. What I would recommend if you encounter workplace discrimination and/or are fired because you have NLD, is that: a) you find a good LD advocacy lawyer, b) you have handy a copy of your most recent diagnostic write-up, and c) have some other official resource that proves that NLD qualifies as an "intellectual or developmental disability." If all that does not work, then hope that you can use some other condition you may have, like anxiety, as a "fallback disability." If you want to find out more about the history of the ADA, go to www.ADAarchive.org.

Q. As an individual with NLD, am I eligible for military service?

Although I personally do not know any NLDers in the service, to the best of my knowledge, there is no law that prevents you from joining if you want to serve. Unlike colleges, however, the military does not have to make accommodations, either for the entrance tests or during service. On the other hand, the structure, rules, and very clear expectations of the military may suit an individual with NLD very well. You yourself and perhaps the recruiting staff will have to determine whether any problems you may have, such as difficulty with visual-spatial skills or adapting to new situations – such as suddenly finding yourself being shipped out to another country – might make service difficult.

These are just some of the questions I've received so far from readers like you and your parents – or are things I've wondered about myself. I welcome any more questions you may have, as well as your input on the ones in this chapter. Please visit my website, www.nldfromtheinsideout.com and let me hear from you.

So how do we going about living a successful life with NLD? Find out in Chapter Seven.

Chapter Seven:
It's a Wonderful Life – Even with NLD

Now that you have read our best tips and strategies for dealing with some of the more challenging aspects of NLD, you may want to think more about your future. What is adult life like when you have a disability?

> *I know that it's hard for you, but it's not always going to be this bad. Some of the symptoms ease up over the years, and you learn to adapt and compensate for your weaknesses, and build on your strengths. Plus, high school sucks for everyone, and life gets better once you get out of high school.*

> *Even if I had known [about having NLD] earlier, I think the maturity of adolescence was required for the type of serious introspection and self-analysis that I have done in the past two to three years.*

Creating a Happy Life for Yourself

From talking with dozens of other young adults with NLD, here is more about what I've learned and you might want to know about creating a full, rich life for yourself. If you are a neurotypical parent reading this, these simple "rules" may be obvious to you. But those of us with NLD don't necessarily grasp them intuitively.

ONE:

You need just **one living being who loves you and whom you love** in return. This can be a parent, sibling, grandparent, aunt, uncle, cousin, or other family member. It can be a best friend or spouse, or anyone else with whom you have a strong and loyal connection. Notice I didn't say "boyfriend" or "girlfriend." If you have a significant other in your life right now, that's great, but that relationship is likely to change as you change and grow. So it's best not to depend on a love-interest as your "one person" unless you are married to them. (And, as many of the survey respondents, whose parents are divorced, know all too well, even marriage isn't necessarily a lifelong relationship any more.)

> *I don't have a lot of friends, but I have one best friend, who has been my best friend since kindergarten. She doesn't have NLD, but she totally "gets" who I am. Plus, my parents, even though we don't always get along, are always here for me.*

Two:

Find at least **one positive and healthy thing you really love to do**. This can be something physical, like a sport, or mental, like doing the *New York Times* Sunday crossword puzzle, or Sudoku, or chess. Or it could be something artistic, like painting, or building miniatures for doll houses. Or musical, like playing in a band, or even just listening to the oldies station for so long that you become an expert on rock music.

> *Be yourself. Find something you love and do it with all your energy.*
>
> *Work and love are both important. But if you had to pick just one, I'd go for work or a hobby every time. Work doesn't forget to call. Work rarely disappoints you. Work doesn't tease you or call you names. If you have a problem with work, the answer depends on you. What you put into your work is pretty much what you will get out. Unlike love, which can be unpredictable.*

Finding one thing you love to do often leads right into the next element of a happy life:

Three:

Find a community where you feel valued and where you belong. This can be related to the one thing you really love to do, or to another passion. Being a valued member of a group you respect and with which you can connect makes you feel good about yourself and about your future.

I attend religious services weekly. When I walk into the Sanctuary, I am greeted by at least 45 people who know me and who make me feel like I am not only welcome there, but that my presence really matters.

When I joined the literary magazine at college, I found myself among a group of like-minded people with a common goal: to publish an irreverent, entertaining journal. I really looked forward to the meetings. I felt welcome and important, especially when my stories got in print.

FOUR:

Find **a way to be productive**. Whether you are studying for a diploma or a degree, working as a bagger in the local supermarket, or volunteering to cook or serve dinner at a homeless shelter, you are giving of yourself and making the world a little bit better. However small your efforts may seem, they really matter. No one on this planet has the exact combination of gifts and talents and strengths that you have. You *can* make a difference in the world – so go do it.

I work at Pet Pals shelter on Saturdays, helping to feed and water the animals, and even clean up the cages and stuff. This is the best part of my week, and I'm always sad and happy at the same time when one of my favorite dogs or kittens gets adopted. I wish I could take them all home with me.

Because of having NLD, I really didn't think that there was any organization that would want me as a volunteer, because my people skills aren't that great. But I was really surprised to find out from my math teacher that if you are good on a computer, there are a lot of organizations that can use your help. She helped me to connect with a local battered women's shelter. I now work in the office two days a week after school, helping them with mailings to donors and entering the gifts into their data base. The next project is they are going to let me work on re-designing their website! I am so happy that I can contribute to a cause I believe in.

FIVE:

Have a dream and work toward it. What do you want to do with your life? Although you may not recognize this right now, those unique talents and gifts can be shared in service to others or parlayed into a career, or both. Perhaps you are one of the lucky ones: you already know that you are a talented artist, or a whiz with computers, or that you have a gentle touch with animals, or that you make the best cupcakes in town:

> *When I was in high school, my parents were so focused on me getting into a "good" college that I didn't think I had the option not to go to college at all. But the one thing that brings me the most joy is baking – everything from simple breads and muffins to fancy party desserts. After spending two miserable years in a college that was all wrong for me, I dropped out and got a job at the local bakery. After a while, the owner urged me to apply to a culinary arts program, so I did, majoring in Baking and Pastry Arts. I'll graduate soon, and already have half a dozen job offers doing what I love best!*

> *My work at the pet shelter has been so satisfying that I am seriously considering going to college, and then on to veterinary school. It would be my dream job to help heal sick or injured animals.*

It is important to take pride in and to celebrate your accomplishments along the way. All the subjects had at least one goal they had reached which greatly improved self-esteem and their view of the world, and actually made them feel happier.

> *One of my favorite [accomplishment]s is that in college so far I've made the Dean's List twice... And to make the Dean's List at this University, you need to have a 3.5 or higher and no incompletes, and full-time status, a minimum of 12 credits. I've also made improvements in social areas too...*

> *After basically flunking out of two colleges, after I got my diagnosis, I entered [a local] community college and graduated with my associates degree* summa cum laude.

I trained for six months for a 10k race for women. Of course I didn't win, not even close, but I finished in a respectable (for me) time. For someone who grew up knowing she was a total klutz, this really changed the way I see myself. I now feel I can do almost anything!

Perhaps you have many different interests and skills, but have not yet discovered the one thing that makes you want to get up and get going in the morning. How can you find it? One tool we have found useful is to spend some time thinking about your life and what you want from it. What does having NLD mean to you? What will it mean as you grow up?

Reflections On Growing Up With NLD

Most of those who contributed to this book have spent some time reflecting on what it means to have NLD. These reflections took many different forms. Most respondents have discussed their condition with others, including parents (65%), siblings or other relatives (30%), friends who have NLD (35%) and friends who do not (39%), teachers (26%), and therapists, counselors, or religious leaders (57%).

These conversations are not always easy or simple:

[I've done] a whole lot of introspection. I have on occasion discussed [having NLD] to a limited extent with parents and friends but it is still extremely uncomfortable for me to do so.

We also spent time in self-reflection, expressing ourselves through journal writing (48%), meditation (17%), song or poetry writing (22%), painting, drawing or sculpture (9%), or through the performing arts (26%). Others reported the following:

Internal self-reflection (reflecting on the nature of my condition without writing anything down).

Learning more about it and educating others.

Discuss with husband.

Learning about NLD and disabilities in general.

Another method of self-reflection – and a good way for us to help others – is to think about and share what we've learned about growing up with NLD. The survey asked: "What would you tell a young friend or relative who just found out they have NLD?" Our answers ranged from the **very specific**...:

> *I'd just give them a PDA and show them how to use it. It would come in handy.*
>
> *Get in LD classes.*
>
> *Try to take the ACT instead of the SAT. When you are applying to grad school, try to find a school that accepts the Miller Analogy Test rather than the GREs – much easier.*
>
> *I would like to add some advice: start at a community college and let them know about your disability, and then go for a 4- year degree.*
>
> *Go to the State Vocational Rehabilitation people for funding for college and help with job finding and coaching after you get out of college.*

...to **the philosophical**...:

> *Try to find a happy medium between blending in with the crowd and going your own way. Social isolation only compounds depression.*
>
> *That everything goes up from here!*
>
> *Just be yourself, and don't worry about the other kids teasing you.*

...to a **combination** of both:

> *I would certainly like to spend more time with them and observe them and hope to be able to give them advice along the way. I probably wouldn't tell them anything initially because I don't want my informing them about their NLD to become a self-fulfilling prophecy. I have been extremely cautious (as much as*

humanly possible) to make absolutely sure that I do not limit myself by talking myself into anything. I have to make sure with several examples that I have been insurmountably limited by a certain element of my NLD.

It's not the end of the world. Get therapy and intervention. Skip classes if you want to. Skip gym. Watch fashions and dress to blend in but don't follow the crowd. You could have it way worse. You can learn to hide NLD, but you'd never be able to hide a wheelchair. NLD is just one tiny part of who you are, and it has nothing to do with your soul or personality. It's just a disability. You'll always be yourself first.

That I have it too. I understand what they are going through and I can help them find ways to compensate through school and finding an advocate to help them out throughout the years, including job hunting.

I would tell them to get interventions immediately with all of the resources they have. The younger they start, the more they'll see improvement. I'd encourage them to be an advocate for themselves and never let their rights be denied. Finally, I'd tell them not to give up hope – things get better as you get older.

The survey also asked: "What do you wish you'd known earlier?" The answers were both poignant and practical:

I wish I had had the diagnosis of NLD when I was younger so that I could have received interventions and a greater understanding of self from a young age.

[I wish I'd known earlier] that I would need things said to me in words.

I would have loved to have known earlier in my childhood that I had NLD because then I could have gotten accommodations and learned how I need to learn.

That I'm not stupid. And I'm not weird for looking at things differently.

That I had [NLD], so teachers could adjust tests, and I wouldn't have had to take a special ed class.

[I wish I'd known] the possible outcomes that could have resulted. What could have happened had I NOT gone into Special Ed. What could have happened had I received a correct diagnosis sooner.

I wish I had known about my various disorders and how they affect me. My ADHD wasn't treated until I was 14, social phobia wasn't treated until I was 17. I wish I had known about NLD, that I wasn't just a total failure.

I don't know … we knew a lot about my disabilities very early on. (They just didn't have a real name.) Maybe that I wasn't really epileptic and didn't need anti-convulsant meds, though.

That I had [NLD], that a lot of the things that happened were not my fault and that there is nothing wrong with me.

I wish I'd known absolutely everything that was going to happen in my life, down to the last second, of course! Then I could expect it! But I'm being facetious. I wish I'd known that it takes a lot to kill a person. You are stronger than you realize. No matter what you're going through, somebody else has it worse. Every second will pass, every hour will pass, every day will pass, eventually.

[I wish I'd known earlier] that I am fine the way I am, that some of the challenges of having NLD will resolve with time, and that my life is what I make of it!

There *is* more to you than your NLD, though sometimes it may not feel that way. The symptoms, limitations, and challenges may feel so overwhelming that it is easy to lose sight of the whole, unique person you are – NLD and all. As you grow to adulthood, it is important to be mindful that things do get better over time for most of us.

Conclusion: What I Learned From Talking to Others With NLD

Mostly, if I could say one thing to others with NLD, it would be to comfort them, to show them that someone has gone before and things have turned out OK.

In the six years I spent working on this project, from doing the research for the psychology paper which led to my thesis which turned into this book, the hundreds of emails from readers I've received and answered, and finally this Second Edition, I found that many of our previous assumptions about NLD were wrong. Difficulty with math seems to be gender-linked, there is no "right-hemisphere disorder," not all Executive Functioning skills are created equal, and the majority of symptoms do tend to improve, to name just a few.

But more importantly, I've found that we can learn a lot by actually *listening* to what people with NLD have to say about their own experiences, thoughts, and feelings. Undiagnosed or misdiagnosed NLD can lead to an enormous waste of human potential. Earlier diagnosis, earlier intervention, and better preparation on the part of parents, therapists, doctors, and schools is needed. Schools need more funding and more teacher training, parents and therapists need more education. Above all else, more tolerance is needed by all concerned, so that those of us with NLD can achieve our full academic, social, occupational, and spiritual potential.

Like every good social scientist, I will end by saying: "more research and funding is necessary." My goal is to research further the themes discussed herein, particularly how the symptoms of NLD and other LDs change over time. Now that this book is finished, I hope to find a doctoral program that is NLD-friendly which will enable me to do this work. In the meantime, I welcome your comments, ideas, questions, stories, and suggestions. You can write to me at www.nldfromtheinsideout.com. Thank you for reading my book. I really look forward to hearing from you.

Michael Brian Murphy

October 2010

Acknowledgements

My grateful thanks to:

The interview subjects and survey respondents, who generously shared their stories.

My mother, Gail Shapiro, for everything, including being a great editor, plus for allowing me to include in Chapter Six all the charts and organizational tools she created as she was raising me.

My Special Education teachers and Disability Services staff members – who rarely get credit for the hard work they do:

Marlene Moskowitz, Ronnie Swain, Evangela Paveloglou, Kathy Trierweiler, Patricia Gavett, Steve Rizzo, Brian Newmark, Joan McGonagle, Judie Picket, Beth Stebe, Sue Batchelder, Mary Caruso, Susan Robinson, Anne Fein, Charles Schneeweis, Rita Heywood, and Sharon DeKlerk.

All my teachers, with a special mention to:

Professor Everett Fox, Professor Diane Harper, Rabbi Lawrence Kushner, Daniel Pellegrini, Dr. Frank Smith, Marcia Tangerini, and Susie Rodenstein.

Those who gave me advice and/or helped contribute to this project:

My grandparents, Arline and Harold Shapiro; Professors David Stevens, James Laird, and Michael Bamberg at Clark University; Katharine Berlin, Catherine Gronewold, Cliff Kolovson, Dr. Sandy Miller-Jacobs, Dr. Scott Sokol, Dr. Nick Dubin, Gayle Alexander, Dan Turnbull, and especially, Gilbert Wolin.

Angela and Richard Hoy and the rest of the Booklocker staff for giving me a shot at success by publishing this book.

And finally, to every one of you who took the time to read this book and to learn more about NLD.

Notes

[1] www.surveymonkey.com.

[2] Joyanne Cobb. Learning How to Learn: Getting Into and Surviving College When You Have a Learning Disability. (Washington, D.C.: Child & Family Press, 2003), 7.

[3] See http://neurodiversity.com/.

[4] Byron P. Rourke. "Questions and Answers: Question #6," Question 6, Answer 6. http://www.nld-bprourke.ca/BPRA6.html.

[5] The Lighthouse Project. "About Lighthouse Project," Lighthouse Project: Providing Occupational Therapy Services for Individuals with Unique Learning Needs. http://thelighthouseproject.com/aboutTLP.html.

[6] Rondalyn Varney Whitney. Bridging the Gap: Raising a Child with Nonverbal Learning Disorder. (New York: Perigee Trade/Penguin Group, 2002).

[7] Doris Johnson and Helmer Mykelbust. Learning Disabilities: Educational Principles and Practices. (New York: Grune & Stratton, 1967), 272.

[8] Byron P. Rourke. Nonverbal Learning Disabilities: The Syndrome and the Model. (New York, London: Guilford Press, 1989).

[9] Wechsler Adult Intelligence Scale® (WAIS). Retrieved from http://www.wilderdom.com/personality/intelligenceWAISWISC.html.

[10] Rourke, 1989, op. cit. Rourke's theory remains essentially the same in his subsequent books: Byron P. Rourke, Darren R. Fuerst. Learning Disabilities and Psychosocial Functioning: A Neuropsychological Perspective. (New York, London: The Guilford Press, 1991); and Byron P. Rourke, Syndrome of Nonverbal Learning Disabilities: Neurodevelopmental Manifestations. (New York, London: The Guilford Press, 1995).

[11] Rourke, 1989, op. cit.

[12] See books Nonverbal Learning Disabilities at Home: A Parent's Guide. (London, Philadelphia: Jessica Kingsley Publishers, 2001); Nonverbal Learning Disabilities at School: Educating Students with NLD, Asperger Syndrome, and Related Conditions. (London, Philadelphia: Jessica Kingsley Publishers, 2002); and articles "Nonverbal Learning Disorders: What to Look For," NLD On The Web!. 1998. http://www.nldontheweb.org/tanguay_3.htm; "NLD = VIQ > PIQ...It Ain't Necessarily So," NLD On The Web!. 1999. http://www.nldontheweb.org/tanguay.htm.

[13] In addition to The Source for Nonverbal Learning Disorders. (East Moline, IL: LinguiSystems, 1997); see www.nldline.com.

[14] See Katherine Stewart, Ph.D. Helping a Child with Nonverbal Learning Disorder or Asperger's Syndrome. (Oakland, CA: New Harbinger Publications, 2002).

[15] Joseph Palombo, LCSW. Nonverbal Learning Disabilities: A Clinical Perspective. (New York, London: W. W. Norton and Company, 2006).

[16] Ibid, 125-143.

[17] Lynda J. Katz, Gerald Goldstein, Sue R. Beers. Learning Disabilities in Older Adolescents and Adults: Clinical Utility of the Neuropsychological Perspective. (New York, Boston, Dordrecht, London, Moscow: Klawer Academic/Plenum Publishers, 2001), 72.

[18] The United States Department of Health and Human Services Centers for Disease Control and Prevention. "Autism Information Center," <u>Department of Health and Human Services Centers for Disease Control and Prevention</u>. http://www.cdc.gov/ncbddd/Autism/.

[19] Gayle Alexander, M.A.Ed. Personal interview, 18 August, 2010.

[20] Nick Dubin, Ph.D.. Personal interview, 16 August, 2010.

[21] Sue Thompson. <u>The Source for Nonverbal Learning Disorders</u>. (East Moline, IL: LinguiSystems, 1997), 167-8.

[22] David Dobbs. "The Gregarious Brain," <u>The New York Times.</u> (July 8, 2007, sec.6), 44.

[23] Howard Gardner. <u>Intelligence Reframed: Multiple Intelligences for the 21st Century</u>. (New York: Basic Books, 2000).

[24] Wechsler Adult Intelligence Scale® – Third Edition (WAIS-III) http://psychcorp.pearsonassessments.com/HAIWEB/Cultures/en-us/Productdetail.htm?Pid=015-8980-727&Mode=summary.

[25] Wechsler Intelligence Scale for Children® – Third Edition (WISC-III) http://psychcorp.pearsonassessments.com/HAIWEB/Cultures/en-us/Productdetail.htm?Pid=015-8979-893&Mode=summary.

[26] Rourke, 1989, op. cit.

[27] Pamela Tanguay. "NLD = VIQ > PIQ...It Ain't Necessarily So," <u>NLD On The Web!</u>. 1999. http://www.nldontheweb.org/tanguay.htm.

[28] Wechsler Adult Intelligence Scale® (WAIS), op. cit.

[29] Alan S. Kaufman. <u>Intelligent Testing with the WISC®-III</u>. Wiley Series on Personality Processes. (New York, Chichester, Brisbane, Toronto, Singapore: John Wiley & Sons, Inc., 1994), 150.

[30] Wechsler Adult Intelligence Scale® – Fourth Edition (WAIS-IV) http://psychcorp.pearsonassessments.com/HAIWEB/Cultures/en-us/Productdetail.htm?Pid=015-8980-808&Mode=summary.

[31] Wechsler Intelligence Scale for Children® – Fourth Edition (WISC®-IV) http://psychcorp.pearsonassessments.com/HAIWEB/Cultures/en-us/Productdetail.htm?Pid=015-8979-044&Mode=summary.

[32] Pamela Tanguay. <u>Nonverbal Learning Disabilities at School: Educating Students With NLD, Asperger's Syndrome and Related Conditions.</u> (London, Philadelphia: Jessica Kingsley Publishers, 2002).

[33] Sylvia S. Mader. <u>Biology</u>. (Boston, Burr Ridge, IL, Dubuque, IA, Madison, WI, New York, San Francisco, St. Louis, Bangkok, Bogotá, Caracas, Kuala Lumpur, Lisbon, London, Madrid, Mexico City, Milan, Montreal, New Delhi, Santiago, Seoul, Singapore, Sydney, Taipei, Toronto: McGraw-Hill Higher Education, 2004), G- 20.

[34] Professor Scott Hendricks. Clark University, class lecture, "Philosophy of Psychology," Psych 241, Fall 2005.

[35] Adapted from Rita Carter. <u>Mapping The Mind</u>. (Berkeley, Los Angeles, London: University of California Press, 1998), 14-17.

[36] Norman Doidge, MD. <u>The Brain That Changes Itself: Stories of Personal Triumph from the Frontiers of Brain Science</u>. (New York: Viking, 2007), 80.

[37] Mader, op. cit., 701.

[38] Ibid.

[39] Ibid., 81.
[40] Ibid., 82.
[41] Rourke, 1989, op. cit.
[42] Carter, op. cit., 37, 115, 129.
[43] Rourke, 1989, op. cit.
[44] Professor David Stevens. Personal conversation, January, 2006.
[45] Doidge, op. cit., 38.
[46] Carter, op. cit., 182.
[47] Laura E. Berk. Infants, Children, and Adolescents. (Boston, New York, San Francisco, Mexico City, Montreal, Toronto, London, Madrid, Munich, Paris, Hong Kong, Singapore, Tokyo, Cape Town, Sydney: Pearson/Allyn and Bacon, 2005), 220-1.
[48] Carter, op. cit., 61, 182.
[49] Eric Jaffee. "Mirror Neurons: How We Reflect On Behavior." Observer: Volume 20, Number 5 (Association for Psychological Science, May 6, 2007), http://www.psychologicalscience.org/observer/getARticle.cfm?id=2167.
[50] Doidge, op. cit., 226.
[51] Louann Brizendine, M.D., The Male Brain: A Breakthrough Understanding of How Men and Boys Think. (New York: Broadway Books, 2010), xvi.
[52] Ibid.
[53] Ibid.
[54] Ibid.
[55] Martin Seligman. Learned Optimism: How to Change Your Mind and Your Life. (New York: Free Press/Simon & Schuster, 1998), 15.
[56] Christopher Peterson, Steven F. Maier and Martin E. P. Seligman. Learned Helplessness: A Theory for the Age of Personal Control. (New York, Oxford: Oxford University Press, 1993).
[57] John Medina. Brain Rules: 12 Principles for Surviving and Thriving at Work, Home and School. (Seattle: Pear Press, 2009), 174.

[58] Ibid., 176.
[59] Ibid., 178-9.
[60] Gretchen Reynolds. "Phys Ed: Can Exercise Moderate Anger?" The New York Times (August 11, 2010). http://well.blogs.nytimes.com/2010/08/11/phys-ed-can-exercise-moderate-anger/?pagemode=print.
[61] Tara Parker-Pope. "Vigorous Exercise Linked With Better Grades." The New York Times (June 3. 2010). http://well.blogs.nytimes.com/2010/06/03/vigorous-exercise-linked-with-better-grades/?pagemode=print.
[62] Ibid., 21-22.
[63] Nick Dubin. Asperger Syndrome and Anxiety: A Guide to Successful Stress Management. (London, Philadelphia: Jessica Kingsley Publishers, 2009).
[64] Cindy Post Senning, Peggy Post, and Sharon Watts. Teen Manners: From Malls to Meals to Messaging and Beyond. (New York: HarperTeen, 2007).
[65] http://www.emilypost.com/children-and-teens.
[66] http://www.rudebusters.com.

[67] Stephen Nowicki, Jr., Ph.D. and Marshall P. Duke, Ph.D. <u>Will I Ever Fit In?: The Breakthrough Program for Conquering Adult Dyssemia</u>. (Atlanta: Peachtree Publishers, 2003).

[68] Editors of Esquire Magazine. <u>Esquire: The Handbook of Style: A Man's Guide to Looking Good</u>. (Hearst Publishers, 2009).

[69] "Internet Dating for the Disabled." <u>The Internet Dating Guide</u>. http://www.theinternetdatingguide.com/disabled_internetdating/.

[70] Nick Dubin, 2009, op. cit., 120.

[71] Lynda Madaras with Area Madaras. <u>The "What's Happening to My Body?" Book for Boys, Revised Third Edition</u>. (New York: Newmarket Press, 2007).

[72] Lynda Madaras with Area Madaras. <u>The "What's Happening to My Body?" Book for Girls, Revised Third Edition</u>. (New York: Newmarket Press, 2007).

[73] Ruth Bell Alexander. <u>Changing Bodies, Changing Lives: Expanded Third Edition: A Book for Teens on Sex and Relationships</u>. (New York: Random House, 1998).

[74] Boston Women's Health Book Collective. <u>Our Bodies, Ourselves: A New Edition for a New Era</u>. (New York: Touchstone, 2005).

[75] Lynn Koegel, Ph.D. and Claire LaZebnik. <u>Growing Up on the Spectrum: A Guide to Life, Love, and Learning for Teens and Young Adults with Autism and Asperger's</u>. (New York: Viking, 2009).

[76] Jonathan Mooney and David Cole. <u>Learning Outside The Lines: Two Ivy League Students With Learning Disabilities And ADHD Give You The Tools</u>. (New York: Fireside, 2000).

[77] Sue Thompson, "Homeschooling and the Child with NLD." <u>NLD On The Web!</u>. http://www.nldontheweb.org/thompson-7.htm.

[78] Larry Berger, Michael Colton, Manek Mistry, Paul Rossi, and Jean Huang. <u>Up Your Score: The Underground Guide to the SAT, 2007-2008 Edition</u>. (New York, Workman Publishing Company, 2006).

[79] The explanations for the SAT, as well as the GRE, TOEFL, and many other standardized tests are found at the ETS homepage: www.ets.org.

[80] Cynthia Simpson and Vicky G. Spencer. <u>College Success for Students With Learning Disabilities: Strategies and Tips to Make the Most of Your College Experience</u>. (Austin: Prufrock Press, 2009).

[81] Andie Parton and Lynn Johnston, <u>Leaving Home: Survival of the Hippest</u>. (Kansas City: Andrews McMeel Publishing, 2003)

[82] Larry Berger and Lynn Harris, <u>Tray Gourmet: Be Your Own Chef in the College Cafeteria</u>. (New York, Lake Isle Press, Inc., 1992).

[83] Cobb, op. cit.

[84] You can search for an Elder Law attorney in your community at the website of the National Academy of Elder Law Attorneys, Inc., a non-profit organization. "Leading the Way in Special Needs and Elder Law." http://www.naela.org/.

[85] Yvona Fast. <u>Employment for Individuals With Nonverbal Learning Disabilities and Asperger's Syndrome: Stories and Strategies</u>. (London and Philadelphia: Jessica Kingsley Publishers, 2006).

86 Chai R. Feldblum, Kevin Barry, Emily A. Benfer. "The ADA Amendments Act of 2008." <u>Texas Journal on Civil Liberties & Civil Rights</u>. (Spring, 2008), 203.

87 National Council on Disability. "Righting the ADA, No. 1: Introductory Paper," The Americans With Disabilities Act Policy Brief Series, (2002). <u>http://www.ncd.gov/newsroom/publications/2002/rightingtheada.htm</u>.

88 Feldblum, Barry, Benfer, op. cit., 202.

89 Ibid., 203.

90 Ibid., 204.

91 Ibid., 238.

Breinigsville, PA USA
15 December 2010
251489BV00002B/39/P